A Cha

By

Adrian Elson

CHAPTER ONE

A CHAMPION LOST

Every so often in life, someone different will come along, as they raise the bar, stand out, appear special.

Barrie Michael Elson lost his life on Tuesday 29th August 1967. He had celebrated his sixteenth birthday just three weeks earlier. He was the reigning National Schoolboy Cyclo-Cross Champion of England, as well as having a plethora of other titles to his name. He had represented Great Britain abroad and won. The press titled him the Coventry 'Whiz Kid'. He was practically unbeatable.

I was four when Barrie died; I only have one memory of him, as he carried me through a wood, blood dripping copiously from a head wound. He was the brother I never had, a person whose entire existence was explained to me via stories, fables, photographs and the heart ache of a Mother. All the medals, jerseys, trophies, press cutting…it was like I was watching a subliminal cine film in sepia, with Barrie as the star, although there were no words and certainly not a happy ending. Yet, he was always there, in the background, his memory, his spirit.

1

I was so very young at the time and so there was no way I could fully assimilate it. Take it all in. Before time, it would move on and hearts - they began to heal and the memories – they began to fade away.

Then one day, I grew up. Although adult hood, if it had taught me anything, it was that life was precious; far too precious for a son, a brother, who now seemed to have been cast into the annals of history. Of course, I could never be certain how the rest of my family felt, but, to me, it wasn't right. It wasn't good enough. I needed to rectify things.

Our Mum had long since died, all the sibling had flown the nest and so that left Dad all on his own. One day, as I walked into his bedroom, I would catch sight of a large black and white framed photograph in a cupboard. It was Barrie! Resplendent in his racing gear as he cruised to yet another victory. Why, every so often, if I thought I couldn't be heard, I'd get the picture out before standing back to admire it.

The photo was of another era, another place, such an amazing successful chapter. The image, so full of life and vigour, genius and skill, in a split second I would feel if he was alive again - invigorated.

Then, just as soon as it had come, the moment was gone. Yet, there it sat, up against a wall in between some discarded vests and shirts - so damn disrespectful as far as I was concerned. For, I just wanted to take it away, release it from its prison. Sure, I could never bring my brother back, but, the least I could do was to display it for a whole world to appreciate once again. I hadn't been able to help Barrie then, but, I wanted to help him now. It was the very least I could do.

I pondered long and hard over what my Father's reaction might be and the can of worms I might be opening. I'd long since taken Barrie's box of memorabilia and burgeoning scrap book of cuttings that chronicled every twist and turn of his amazing short career. However, as it was, he would raise no objection, although I remembered sensing an air of indifference in his attitude.

I didn't care, as now, I'd got the photo and I was going to put it somewhere it could be seen, somewhere it would be revered once again.

I work from home and so I put it on my office wall. Now, everyday, I look up and I can see Barrie out of the saddle, so supreme, a suffering Chris Dodd on his wheel struggling to keep up, my brother so resplendent in the famous blue and gold of his Coventry Road Club jersey, black woollen shorts and ankle length socks. As I write this book, it's still there now, no longer hidden away, buried in the morass of a Father's junk. Barrie Elson, a cycling superstar.

Furnished with the photograph, I looked to bolster his memory further, as I sponsored a youth event with a first prize that made it the richest race on the calendar. Yet, as the years moved on, then even that wouldn't seem quite enough, as it began to become old school. Sure, he was being remembered, but, I felt it was no more than me now giving a short speech before a race, along with the odd photo of the winner on a podium, as he clasped hold of the trophy and his bounty once again.

3

No, as far as I was concerned, Barrie deserved more than this, much more, indeed, something ever lasting. While basically, I needed a kick up the backside to implement it, but what?

Then one day, I would be given the most horrendous news: Charlie Craig had died.

CHAPTER TWO

By now, I was in my mid fifties and with my own cycling career long gone, I was being paid to do on course cycle commentary on cyclo-cross. A few weeks earlier, I had commentated at the Macclesfield Super Cross. The race is renowned for its generous prize money, whilst it attracts the top cyclo-cross names in the country. It was there, that I would interview one of the most unique young riders, indeed, people that I have ever met.

His name was Charlie, Charlie Craig, the son of Nick Craig, an ex-Elite Cyclo-Cross Champion who was still at the top of his game. As for his son, he was following in his Father's footsteps and had already amassed an impressive palmarès despite his young age.

I knew Nick vaguely; I'd interviewed him at the previous year's race, while in my own racing days I'd purchased one of his old mountain bikes off his ex-team manager Gary Coltman. It was a superb Diamondback, with top of the range components and airplane tubing, which meant it weighed in at twenty one pounds (extremely light for a mountain bike). The bike had been all around the world with Nick and I spoke to him about this, after I stopped him in his tracks as he practiced on the course for a major cyclo-cross race in Cheltenham one year. You know, I'm still not sure what I was thinking of, as he was a top racer, busy preparing, but, on calling him over, he would gladly come to a halt before the conversation ensued. Back then, I was a complete nobody (probably still am) and I was slightly in awe of him, but, we spoke in detail about it for at least five minutes, before, suddenly, he was gone. My overriding memory though: what a nice guy!

Back in Macclesfield and in the youth race (I hate that terminology) that had just taken place; Charlie had been unlucky to lose in a sprint finish to an aspiring Lewis Askey (he would go on to win the Schoolboy pursuit title in 2017). They had been neck and neck all the way through and now, Charlie was coming across (somewhat reluctantly) to tell me all about it.

You know, I'm not sure what it was, why, even when I look back now I still can't quite put my finger on it. As somehow, he was different. For he had a charm, a grace, a definite presence that far superseded someone of his age. Indeed, any age. As his eyes, they just glowed. Such was the affect on me, I remembered after the interview feeling honoured to have met him.

However, that was three weeks ago and, in the meantime, Charlie had won the Silver Medal in the National Championships at Bradford, again losing out in a sprint finish, this time to Ben Tulett (he would go on to become the World Junior Cyclo-Cross Champion the next year at Valkenburg, Holland). I was doing another race at Alcester in Warwickshire and as I waxed lyrical as the senior riders got under way, my good friend Alix came across to ask me if I had heard the news about Charlie.

I would have no idea what she was talking about, what news about Charlie? It was then that she informed me that he had gone to bed on the Friday night (it was now Sunday) and never woken up again.

Her words would strike me rigid. Commentating was out of the question, as I just stood there, trying to come to terms with the fact that this young lad, this guy that I had thought so special, had so much to live for…was not with us any more. In a second my heart would go out to Charlie's Father, but then Barrie would enter my head, the loss, indeed the whole damn similarity of it all.

I attended the church in Derbyshire for Charlie's funeral. Later that day, during the wake, I gave Nick a medal of Barrie's that he won at the National Youth week at Crystal Palace in 1967 (Barrie won overall). Amongst a crowd of people and as I struggled to get my words out, I wasn't even sure he was taking it all in, but, I wanted him to have it, something of Barrie's to give to Charlie.

A few days later, the events of the day still fresh in my mind, I would sit transfixed as I watched a video of Charlie on You Tube, as he trained on his mountain bike with the effort all set to music. It seemed Charlie was quite the film maker, as I'd watched a similar one he'd produced of his brother Tom as he won a Junior National Trophy race.

The music Charlie had chosen this time, however, seemed so apt, so succinct. It gelled with the breath taking scenery as he rode through the woods, a picture of style, before right at the very end he leaped into the air on his bike into a beguiling sun set. That was Charlie.

Charlie was so special that he was never going to be forgotten and through his Dad, his Mum Sarah, along with his elder brother, as well as all their friends his memory would live on. 'Ride for Charlie' events took place as literally hundreds of cyclists took to the hills, Charlie Van der Craig wristbands were produced, whilst at the World Championships the GB Junior's dedicated their performances to him as they crossed the finish line hands pointing to the air.

For my small part, I had a medal cut in Charlie's memory. Alix's daughter Lauren (Beany) presenting it for me at the 2017 Midland Cyclo-Cross Championships in Worcester to the winner of the Youth race, Daniel Barnes. It simply said: Charlie.

And yet, that still left Barrie. Why, it was never meant to be a competition between the two of them. God knows they were both amazing individuals and yet, every so often, I'd think: what about Barrie?

Sure, my brother was from another age and he had been revered. The myriad of letters of sympathy my Mum and Dad received bore testament to that. Nevertheless, there was no touch of a button global communication, as anyway, I was too young to remember it all, and so, I wanted to put the record straight. Just in case.

But again, what to do? Before suddenly it hit me: write a book! Simple? Although, I so wanted to do Barrie justice. To leave no stone unturned. Except then, I would think to myself: did I really want to conduct a plethora of interviews, troll through a thousand archives, only to come up with a stack of facts and opinions of people who were never that close to him, certainly not as biologically close as a younger brother who held him in such high esteem was anyway. No, if I was going to write it, it would be from my perspective. For after all, it was me who was still carrying the torch. While it would be my chance to complete what Barrie had started; to finally drive him over a finish line. In short, it was the least his legacy and class deserved.

So, here I am today. Or should I say tonight, for my day job has disappeared into the ether. I'm sat amongst a mass of diaries, letters, cycling magazines and who knows what else; a thousand memories of Barrie from people who came across him over the years drilling through my head (boy did I take it on board at the time, but, like I say, I didn't want to conduct interviews) as I seek to tell a story, with my brother looking down at me from a wall.

I will do my very best Barrie, just as you always did.

CHAPTER THREE

"BOY CYCLE STAR'S DEATH –
JUNCTION 'DANGEROUS'"

Tuesday 29th August 1967, 7 pm

As the last realms of 'All you need is Love' rang out from his sister's bedroom, Barrie changed into his Coventry Road Club kit and made his way out of the house, to get aboard his bicycle. He was just sixteen and had been racing for nearly four years.

Earlier, he'd arrived home after another day's work as an apprentice plumber (he'd only been there just over a month). Barrie was fastidious at his job (a later letter of condolence from his employer confirmed this); however, it seems he had harboured ambitions to be a hair dresser. Perhaps, considered a bit too gay for the day, especially in the eyes of his Father - Derrick (Bodger) Elson, who had served his country in Palestine and who knew all there was to know about bigotry if he felt that way inclined. (How he got the name Bodger is debatable even to this day.)

Checking the bike's tyres, he wheeled it out of the back garden, before cocking a leg over its frame and making his way out onto the open road. His destination: the 'bash'.

10

Every Tuesday and Thursday night, racing cyclists met for the training run from hell, where the hammer went down early and if you couldn't keep up- then tough. For, in the days before heart meters and power cranks, this is where you learnt your trade; how to suffer, how to close gaps, but, above all how to stay on a wheel, when all your body wanted to do was keel over and die. Train hard, race easy as Barrie's Dad used to say.

Most of the group consisted of Coventry Road Club riders; strong, classy men, just about to impose themselves on the world of cyclo-cross. The likes of Daryl Brassington, Olly Nagle and Chris Dodd winning National Championships in consecutive years in the late sixties and early seventies. A feat never achieved before by one cycling club, or, since.

The King amongst them, however, and already a multiple National Champion in his own right, was John Atkins (he'd eventually go on to win thirteen National titles). John was someone Barrie aspired to, although, when it came to idols that had been bestowed upon Tommy Simpson. He had been taken from us only a month earlier on a tortuous stage (thirteen) of the Tour de France as the peloton climbed Mont Ventoux. The amphetamines found in Simpson's system, tarnishing Barrie's image of a man who he had looked up to and followed for so long. Not anymore.

John, however, was different. Although he had raced abroad many times representing Great Britain, or, chasing the lucrative start money (he would get one hundred pounds to ride a race in 1971) he was still UK based and lived in Coventry. Any training or events had to fit around his job on the production line of the MG motor company. (John bought an MG from new that year for five hundred pounds.)

As he took in the fresh autumnal air, Barrie would no doubt have thought about the coming cyclo–cross season (1967/68) that was due to start the very next month. It was his first year riding as a junior (competitors had to be between sixteen and eighteen years of age) and after dominating the schoolboy ranks (riders under sixteen) the consensus of opinion stated that he'd do the same at the older level.

To get to the meeting point of the ride, Leamington Road in Coventry, Barrie would have to travel no more than six miles. Which, given the terrain and his fitness, would take about twenty five minutes if taken at a steady pace (he'd make it steady as he knew what torture was in store once the group got underway). It included Craven Avenue to get him out of the estate, Binley Road and then St James Lane, before turning right onto London Road. He'd then turn left on to Abbey Road (Whitley Abbey School would go on to be a renowned cyclo-cross venue) and then move onto Daventry Road before reaching his destination.

7.01pm

Barrie takes a left off Craven Avenue onto Binley Road. It's a route he knows well; his Mum and Dad having moved the family to the brand new sprawling

12

estate of Binley Woods (about seven miles from Coventry city centre) in 1965, as they sought to make a better life for their family. The modern houses, with front and back gardens, were a long way from the virtual two up – two down they'd left behind.

7.07pm

Another left to negotiate now as he turns onto St James Lane. While he's about to skirt the district of Willenhall (a run down part of the city) with a culture of drugs and crime, it had some how missed out on the City of Coventry's manufacturing boom of the 50's and 60's. But, he's feeling good, legs turning well.

7.14pm

Nearly at the end of the road now and the traffic is light, especially when compared with the roads of today. An area famous for its car production, including the iconic Jaguar; yet this is an era where car ownership is classed as a privilege, rather than a right. So, Barrie's journey is unhindered as he prepares for the onslaught which is to come.

7.15pm

Ten minutes to go before Barrie meets the lads and he's got a lot to catch up on. There's no e-mail, or mobile phones and so talking face to face is at a premium. It's the eve of the cyclo-cross season and he's going riding with the main protagonists. This year is an important one, as he'll be competing with the seniors in most of the races (in the 60's Junior riders generally only had a few autonomous races to take part in) and Barrie's keen to know just how close he can get to John Atkins. For Atkins has raised the bar and Barrie is determined to see if he can match it (Barrie gave himself two years in which to beat John).

Dabbing his brakes slightly, before glancing over his right hand shoulder, Barrie begins to move over to the right hand side of the road, as he prepares to turn right onto London Road (a major arterial route leading to the heart of the city). London Road could be busy, but, not that busy and especially not on a quiet sunny Tuesday evening with rush hour now well and truly over. Why, even if it was, it held no fear for Barrie, for he was a skilled bike rider. He'd already ridden thousands of miles in his short career and had never so much as had a 'close one'. The world was his oyster, the press, along with anyone who knew anything about cycling, believed he was going all the way to the very top. He was literally living the dream. A master of his own destiny, and then, suddenly, the van honed into view, a second later and everything would change forever.

CHAPTER FOUR

"ELSON STRIDES OUT"

It is said that champions are born rather than made. However, given Barrie's genetic blue print, then perhaps he fell into the latter of the two categories.

Okay, so he had an Aunt on his Father's side that had been selected for the 1956 Melbourne Olympics swimming team (apparently her parents refused to let her go). Although, that said, there wasn't an obvious characteristic that said, "Hey! This is the next Brian Robinson!"

For when it came to Barrie, he'd been a sickly child, a constant problem with his bowels and stomach leading the specialist to pronounce one day, to a rather disbelieving Mother, that her "son had the insides of an old man of ninety and would never be good for anything!'

His parents wouldn't fair much better. They were both smokers (his Dad eventually giving up after panting furiously running after a bus), whilst when it came to his Mum, I don't think she had merited any sort of athletic performance in her entire life.

His Father, panting aside, had at least gained some success on the track (where the competitors compete on an oval circuit). Many was the time he would wax lyrical, as he told of how he'd given the stars of the day such as Lutz Durlacher (a Commonwealth medallist) a run for their money at the Butts Cycle Stadium in Coventry, as they competed for yet another four hundred and forty yard sprint. Although, it appeared his career had been blighted (according to his Dad) because of him befriending a rider called Johney Hathaway, which in turn stopped him being the next Reg Harris (a multiple World Track Sprint Champion who frequented the Butts on many a Monday night, blond in tow, before entertaining a rapturous crowd of over ten thousand people). For Hathaway was a long distant cycling record holder (he eventually went on to record the fastest time for a coast to coast crossing of America) and his endless training rides with Bodger, would soon put paid to any last embers of speed in his legs.

Indeed, one Saturday afternoon, in the middle of February, after working that morning (the average working week in those days was forty five hours) they took themselves off to Bournemouth for the weekend (it was only a hundred and twenty miles after all!). Into a howling gale on the journey back, on spotting the signs for Coventry, Johney would suggest they take a detour to Banbury, just to make it up to the round one hundred and fifty. Johney's riding partner's reply left him in no doubt as to just what he could do with his ride.

Born the eldest of four children on August the 7th 1951 in Gulson Road Hospital, Coventry, this made Barrie a 'Coventry kid' as it was inside the City walls. At the time, his Mum and Dad were living in a ramshackle caravan park near the city centre. Derrick, demobbed from the army in 1947, he had met his Mum Jean (she always insisted on being called Jane, even scribbling the name in pen on Barrie's birth certificate) at a dance not long after. Of Irish decent (McGrath) it would turn out to be a whirlwind romance, although totally objected to by her Catholic parents who could see no reason why their daughter would want to court someone of another faith (I'm not sure if his Dad had any leaning what so ever). So, with pressure mounting, Derrick and Jean eloped to Scotland to get married, dragging two complete strangers off the street to witness it. However, it would be her parents who exacted the last laugh, as they spirited away their grandchild (Barrie) to be baptised a Roman Catholic.

Growing up, Barrie could be a mischievous child. He had a love of the outdoors, no more so than when he used to go to Silverstone with his Dad. Scurrying at the back of the stands, he'd amass a small fortune as he gathered up the loose change from people's pockets above, as they lay back in their seats.

Later in life, a lack of physique encouraged bullying. Although keeping this to himself for a long time (he did a lot of that), one day he would suddenly blurt it all out to his concerned Father. His Dad (ex-military) would advise his son to get each one of the gang on their own before exacting his revenge.

Departing the bus one evening, from yet another day at work, Derrick would spot Barrie in the distant, in mortal combat with another boy much bigger than himself. Running at break neck speed, to avert the consequent beating, he would discover on arrival that it was in fact his son who was on top, as the bigger boy begged for mercy (he was never bullied again).

Barrie was a clever lad (although his examination results on leaving school hardly bear this out), who it seems was held in some esteem by his Head Master, Mr Foster, at the senior school he attended, Wolston High School, near Rugby. A leaving letter of reference from the gentleman stated the following:

"Barrie had entered in the fourth year and stayed on to take the fifth year course (whatever that was supposed to mean). His English and Maths were average, as well as being average in Geography (not sure why he didn't group them altogether). One afternoon a week we have released him to attend the East Warwickshire College where he undertook a plumbing course. He has been a quiet well balanced pupil, reliable as a prefect (prefect eh!) and he has been reasonably industrious over his work. (Now comes the best bit.) He played games and won the Senior Cross Country but of course his greatest achievements have been in cycling for he is the National Boys Champion in cyclo-cross. He should prove a dependable and well balanced employee." (Well he was right on that score.)

However, getting back to his younger years (he was eleven by now) and like I say, he had not been well, before one day and totally out of the blue, he would calmly announce that he wanted to start cycle racing.

18

As it was, Barrie had always taken an interest in sport and in the stacks of old photos I have in front of me now, there are lots of pictures of him on bikes. Although, there are just as many of him cuddling our many family pets, so perhaps a career in a Veterinary profession might have been pertinent too!

CHAPTER FIVE

A son's revelation would prove music to a Father's ears. Not renowned for being the most diligent of Dads and quite exacting when he wanted to be, Barrie's sudden convergence to a sport he'd long since left behind meant that once more, the name of 'Elson' might have a chance of becoming synonymous when it came to breaking through into the annals of a cycling history (every Father is allowed to dream). And yet, that was a long way down the road. First, would come the beating!

Anyone who has endeavoured to take up a sport competitively (especially cycle racing) and unless they are a pure genius, will know what I'm referring too. Sure, the majority of people have at one time or other ridden a bicycle, but, the hard bit comes when you try to up the speed! Muscle groups, lungs, they all need years of acclimatising before you finally get the finished article (some experts say up to ten thousand hours). Even then, some still find it hard. For, it wasn't that Barrie wasn't good, but more so, that he was young and rather small for his age. As a result, and like all aspiring racers, he would have several pasting inflicted upon him by the older riders. But, it was good character building…or so they say.

Undaunted, Barrie started to serve his cycling apprenticeship, as he tried his hand at time trials, circuit racing, track and cyclo-cross. Money was tight in the household and so his Dad had to literally beg, steal and borrow to ensure that his protégée had the tools he needed.

For the new aspiring rider, his Sundays were now reserved for the club run. He would join lots of other budding cyclists all with the same purpose in mind. As they rode steadily down country lanes side by side, his Father, resplendent in his plus fours as they looked forward to the Sunday 'tea' stop. In the week, any training rides with his Dad resulted in all out sprints for every sign post (his Father was virtually unbeatable). It's interesting to note that even in his formative year's Barrie accumulated a decent mileage. Barrie's diary states four thousand, one hundred and twenty miles in 1963 and four thousand, four hundred miles in 1964 and with his Dad now back in the sport he was being pushed physiologically every time they went out.

It would be cyclo-cross that Barrie would eventually excel at, and yet, even then, the track and the circuit racing were becoming contributory factors towards this. His Dad knew exactly how to use a track bike and he'd pass this experience on to his son as he learnt positioning and how to read a race. Furthermore, the low fixed gear (probably about sixty six inches) would contribute to a fluent, almost effortless riding style.

This invariably took place at the Butts (where Derrick excelled). The circuit racing would encourage race craft, along with the ability to recover quickly from hard efforts, as well as being able to sprint. More importantly though, Barrie's body was now getting used to the 'pounding' of racing, as his 'muscle memory' database began to be built up.

As I mentioned previously, in the 60's there were no such things as power metres, or heart monitors, available to the public. So, riders were very much left to their own devices. Any training regimes that did exist were usually passed down through the generations, as individuals adhered to tried and tested techniques. Unlike today, when training data can be analyzed on a lap top, competitors relied on 'feel' whilst any 'peaking' for an event, was more a case of luck rather than because of careful tapering.

It was the same when it came to diet. Forget your 'five a day', as riders were more inclined to eat what they fancied. It wasn't that long after the cessation of rationing and so perhaps food was seen in a different light. Mick Stallard (an ex-National Senior Champion) swore by the benefits of his pre-race pie and chips the night before he captured yet another title.

So, Barrie would comply with a lot of the rhetoric, getting the miles in, racing here and there and eating what was put in front of him so he was ready to go again. It wasn't rocket science, but then again, it didn't need to be as it was what everyone else was doing. Whilst the only TUE (therapeutic use exemption) that concerned Barrie, was Maths on a Tuesday morning!

When it came to the research for this book, I was aided by the fact Barrie left a lot of diaries, although he didn't complete a detailed account of his racing until he was fourteen. In the meantime, I was left with the odd photograph from a newspaper cutting and the memories of his Father (as he filled me in on the finer points) as we undertook yet another walk with the family dog many years after Barrie's death.

There's a memorable photograph of Barrie (in the Coventry Evening Telegraph from 1963) astride his machine at the Butts as the schoolboys take part in an elimination race/devil take the hindmost (when the rider in last place has to drop out at the end of every lap). It's a significant picture of Barrie, as it shows him at the start of his career, all fresh faced and eager, but with such a small stature, that you can only just pick him out against the older much bigger boys in the race. Although, when you look at his face, well, you can see the concentration, the where with all. Then, when you look into his eyes, you see a soul that says I don't want to win…I need to win. That was Barrie alright.

But, like I say, he had to learn and Dad would tell the story of when Barrie rode one of his first circuit races at Dartmouth Park in Birmingham. It was a horrendous day, as the sky deposited its contents onto the field. While as the leaders came through, glad too finish, there was no sign of Barrie. Many minutes later and looking like what his Dad described as a drowned rat, appeared his son, as he struggled valiantly to the line (yet more character building).

Finally, to add more grist to his mill, he would partake in reliability trials (where you have a set time to cover a set distance). In this instance, I came across a certificate that recorded fifty miles in four hours dated the 21st February 1965. I even unearthed a Cycling

Proficiency test certificate (this was given out in the day, to people who had proven they could master the basics of riding a bike safely on the road). I'm pretty sure Barrie passed with flying colours.

CHAPTER SIX

"FATHER AND SON – FOURTH IN TRIAL"

The early years: 1965 onwards

Barrie had been racing now for two years. He had shown some promise, but, had hardly pulled up any trees. Having said that, unlike today, when virtually every age category is catered for (some of the best racing I have ever commentated on has involved the under 12's), back then, you learnt the hard way; as riders took it in turns to apply yet another nail into an aspiring career.

But, when the going gets tough, the tough get going and Barrie's upbringing had furnished him with stacks of resilience. Whilst his Father was never going to settle for second best; so, he continued, riding, racing, resting and reading the 'Cycling' magazine every Thursday night (once his Dad had finished with it). There was no wall to wall cycling on television in those days. In fact, there was practically none and so the greats of the day developed a sort of 'mystique' as a young boy sat wide eyed just dreaming of 'the day'.

As I look through Barrie's records now, then I don't have to rely on the scarcest of diaries anymore, as I have his events log to refer too, a green embossed book that details the following:

Time trials:
DISTANCE, DATE, NAME OF EVENT, WINNER & HIS TIME, COURSE, BARRIE'S TIME

He would use roughly the same format for the circuit races and track, whilst 'cross' stipulated the following:

DATE, NAME OF EVENT, BARRIE'S PLACING, WINNER

Time trials:

29th April 1965, K41, a club ten mile time trial, Barrie is thirteen.

These days (even in a club event) athletes will turn up with machines that look like they've landed from outer space. With serrated edges and the lightest of components, turbo trainers and gels at the ready, no one even considers going to a start line without their legs being lathered in liniment.

However, in Barrie's day, things were very different, and he certainly didn't buck the trend. Very often his warm up consisted of riding to the event, whilst any ambition to be 'aero' would be achieved by him wearing his racing hat back to front. Competing on his steel framed machine, lugs and cotter pins aplenty (bike components!), his time was a respectable twenty seven minutes and fifty four seconds. Not bad for the course (it had a slow road surface with a few minor climbs), while the winner, Dave Miller (a senior rider) would finish in a time of twenty four minutes and two seconds, which in its day was bloody good.

It was then time for a cup of tea, a good natter, before getting off home before it got dark. Very much like today.

NB: Dave remains a family friend. Indeed, he presented Barrie's cup on the 50th anniversary of his passing, to the winner Lewis Askey at the West Midland Championships in Worcester.

Circuit races:

10th April 1965, Dartmouth Park, Birmingham

If only to back up his Dad's story (partly) Barrie's entry in his log details the event. Indeed, he mentions the wet, along with the fact his gear jammed, and it was fast. His placing: 14th. So, either there weren't many riding, or, his Father's recollections were some what clouded (pardon the pun).

Cyclo-cross: 1965/66

I, also, came across a couple of creditable performances at cyclo-cross.

In September 1965 (he was just fourteen) he achieved a notable placing of second, in an event at Bromsgrove, won by D. Holmes of the Birmingham Wheelers. By now Barrie's weekly mileage was getting higher. He had started riding to school in Wolston (it was a journey of about eight miles there and back) which also included a decent sized climb.

Yet, better was to come. Riding in only his second event that season, organised by the Velo Club Central, he would achieve fourth place to Geoff Shaw of the Wolverhampton Wheelers (at the time he was the reigning National Schoolboy Champion). Okay, so the placing wasn't as good as his first race, but, the recognition he received afterwards, would knock it into a cocked hat.

His Father was working as an aircraft fitter. It involved long arduous hours as he sought to keep a roof over his families' heads. Thursday morning, however, broke the monotony. For Thursday, was the day he collected the 'Cycling' magazine from the local newsagents. This was 1965 and all aspiring cyclists and fans relied on the 'comic' (as it was also known, in fact still is) as the main port of call, for all the cycling news and headlines of the day.

Furthermore, when it came to the front cover, you had to be well sought after or successful, to get a look in. Summer editions became the domain of the likes of Barry Hoban, Tommy Simpson or Beryl Burton...whilst in the winter it was John Atkins or Mick Stallard. And yet, on this occasion, then who should be sharing centre stage, with his picture on the front cover, but, his son, Barrie! Barrie occupied the left hand side of the page, and hill climber Ron 'Zebra' Martin the right. The caption read:

"Barry (they spelt his name wrong) Elson, Coventry Road Club, showed an elegant step climbing style (the picture is of him climbing the steps bike in hand) at Hadley Stadium but was still not good enough to win the Schoolboys Cyclo-Cross event based on the track (Hadley Stadium was primarily a track cycling venue surrounded by woods)."

Meanwhile, his Dad was completely spell bound, as he struggled to take in what he was looking at (novice racing cyclists just didn't make the cover of the 'Cycling').

Yet, was Barrie's picture some sort of foresight on the part of someone on the editorial staff? Barrie would go on to grace the journal many more times in his career, even winning its prestigious 'Cyclist of the Month' award. But, for now, he was still an aspiring fourteen year old. However, the building blocks were now starting to be put in place.

It's impossible to say, if there was a point in Barrie's cycling career that set him on the path to glory. Although, in a Father's eyes, it was the cycle touring holiday to Cornwall he took with his son in the summer of 65 that finally set things in motion. "It was the constant pounding he took each day that made the difference and hardened him off" exclaimed a Father (probably after his son had won everything there was too win by then anyway). However, those were the days of basic training techniques, while the famous Tour Champion Fausto Coppi would state: "ride a bike, ride a bike, ride a bike"; and that's what they did. Throughout the Coventry Holiday Fortnight (this is when all the factories in the town shut down) day after day in the saddle. His Dad may well have had a point; for after all, he was only in his late thirties and was a strong rider in his own right. Barrie on the other hand, was still a relatively frail individual and would suffer on a daily basis. Derrick noted, however, that Barrie never got dropped.

As I delved deeper into my brother's box of memorabilia, I came across a piece of his school work where he details the holiday. His writing is almost Dickensian in its style, with big swirling strokes, it is extremely neat. According to the essay, they got all their stuff together on the Saturday, checked their bikes out on the Sunday and then on Monday 26th of July 1965 they set off, their plan to stay in Youth Hostels.

Like I say, Dad always claimed it was that tour that made the difference. And yet, as I dug further into the box, I also read that they had been on other touring holidays on previous years (Mum and Dad had very little money and I don't recall us ever having a family holiday in the 60s); Wales being one of their favourite destinations. Although, the fable said it was the Cornwall trip that made the difference. So, I was happy to go along with that.

CHAPTER SEVEN

"ELSON STRIDES OUT"

Cyclo-cross season: 1965 – 66

Cyclo-cross is a cycling discipline where the riders compete over several laps. Each lap is usually about a mile in length, which can include woodland, road sections and grass. Competitors may also be required to run with their machines. It was thought that the sport originated as far back as the beginning of the 20th century when French soldiers used their bikes to cross fields more quickly.

3rd September 1965, Bromsgrove: 2nd
Winner: D. Holman

As he prepared for his first cyclo-cross race of the season, Barrie was only just fourteen. By now though he had the best part of two seasons racing under his belt and he was becoming fine tuned to the discipline. His bike handling was getting better, his recovery from efforts more reliable, whilst the Coventry Road Club (the club he rode for) were right behind him when it came to support. Such was their foresight that they established a steering committee of four seniors and three schoolboys, which focused on attracting young riders to the sport of cyclo-cross (it was still a relatively new concept with the first National Championship having been held only ten years earlier at Welwyn Garden City).

23rd October 1965, Velo Club Central: 4th
Winner: G. Shaw

In somewhat a basic fashion (bearing in mind Barrie was only still only fourteen) he illustrated that he was taking his sport seriously, when on a plain piece of paper, I found the following:

One hour training session (this would have been the ideal duration for a rider of his age and size to train for):

<u>Running</u>
It would be important to practice this, to get the body used to the effort. The muscle groups used for both cycling and running are quite different. In the 60's the percentage of a race given over to running was far greater than it is today, whilst at times, organisers went out of their way to find the muddiest field or deepest river to cross.

<u>Riding</u>
This went without saying, the more you rode, the stronger you became. However, as a schoolboy, you had to be careful not to over train. Multiple National Champion Paul Watson informed me years later, that it was better to train rather than to strain.

32

Getting off and on

In this case the bike. Developing an efficient and fast technique could save you seconds each lap. There are so many facets that go to make up the 'cross' rider, but without technique you are nothing.

Carry bike

Again, it was important to develop a style of carrying the bike that enabled control and aided breathing. I've never seen a picture of my brother carrying a bike over his shoulder, but, I was led to believe it was unique.

Fast starts

Crucial in cyclo-cross when racers went from the gun, if you were left behind, you might never get back. Therefore, it was important to have the right gear engaged, as well as keeping a close eye on the starter.

Jumping with bike

In this case, I presumed he meant bunny hoping (where a rider flicks the front wheel up in the air before landing and then repeating it with the rear wheel). This could be used to negotiate planks, or traversing logs; so, get it right and you saved time, get it wrong and you were down the bike shop on a Monday morning buying a new bottom bracket!

Press ups 30
Press ups are always good for the cardiovascular system, which in turn is vital to the aspiring 'cross' rider where the effort is constantly changing.

Bed time, 10 o'clock
Obtaining the right amount of sleep is so important to allow the 'worked' body to repair.

As I say, basic stuff, but in his mind, he was leaving nothing to chance.

31ˢᵗ October 1965, Rugby RCC: 3th (this is how Barrie wrote it) Winner: R. Mear

I would unearth a certificate detailing the fact he won a pound note for his efforts!

13ᵗʰ November 1965, Velo Club Central: 7ᵗʰ (no winner listed)

27ᵗʰ November 1965, Elizabethan CC: 6th Winner: D. Swinerton

4ᵗʰ December 1965, De Laune National Schoolboys Cyclo-Cross Championships: 10ᵗʰ Winner: G. Shaw

Until I looked through Barrie's press cutting in depth, I had no idea he'd ridden another Schoolboy Cyclo-Cross Championship. Yet, there it was, in his

34

log, along with a press cutting to back it up. One of his rivals Ray Pinder (Coventry Cycling Club) who went on to finish 3rd in the following year's Championships, finished ahead of Barrie in eighth place. The Championship was won for the second year by Geoff Shaw (it was only the second running of the Schoolboy Championship). When one takes into consideration, that at the time, Barrie was only fourteen and a half, his final placing was good. While the next year, he knew that a lot of his opposition would be moving up to the junior ranks.

When I made my comeback to the sport as a veteran (riders over forty years of age) I took part in an event in Birmingham, along with Pinder, who was also making a comeback. I still remember the whole experience being rather cathartic, to me anyway, almost as if I was reliving the past, with me as Pinder's competition now rather than Barrie. The question was: could I beat him?

I was in pretty good form at the time and it was no contest. Although, I knew that Pinder would have been far better in his day.

At the end of the race, I went over and shook his hand and explained I was Barrie's brother. We seemed to click straight away, whilst he went on to say that he had an old cine film of Barrie that he was trying to upload to a CD. God, I was so thrilled when I heard that, I'd never seen my brother ride, indeed, I didn't even know what his voice sounded like. I never did get to see the finished CD, but, I live in hope to this day.

Looking at the log, it appeared the events were few and far between (of course that could have been dictated by the amount of events he was able to get to). However, when it comes to today, especially due to the growth of the regional leagues, it's possible to ride two events every weekend if you want to. That said I would come across an article detailing a double victory on the same day by Mick Ives.

12th March 1966, Warwickshire Championship: 9th
Winner: G. Shaw

This was Barrie's final event of the season; and yet, it's notable by the date. These days the sport of cyclo-cross finishes in January, whilst March is reserved for the early season reliability trials and hilly time trials. Personally, I've never really understood this; with the season starting in the September, people are normally left melting in the heat, so surely a season between October and March would be much more beneficial.

The 1965/66 season now over, an analysis of Barrie's results, especially given his age, showed it had been a solid period with a few highlights. He'd never finished outside the top ten and had achieved a second place. Barrie was learning as he went along and getting better race by race. The best however…was yet to come.

CHAPTER EIGHT

"BARRIE ELSON UPHELD ENGLAND'S PRIDE"

After a short break to recoup, Barrie would start racing again. In May of 1966 he claimed the Bronze Medal in the Coventry Divisional Road Race Championships, Ray Pinder beating him again to win the Gold.

Barrie also took part in the National Youth Week at Crystal Palace, under BCF (British Cycling Federation) rules. The event for aspiring young riders of the day, it consisted of a whole host of competitions including track, time trials and circuit races. Barrie wouldn't finish in the medals. Even so, he did enough to be recognised; as just two months later, my brother was picked for the Great Britain team taking part in the 10th running of the Schoolboy Tour of West Brabant in Holland (22nd to 28th of July 1966). It would be the first time Great Britain entered a team.

A showcase for young talent, it attracted six hundred eager individuals from across Europe. Using a handicapping system, they would pit their wits against each other, gaining points across a multitude of disciplines, including cyclo-cross (even though it was July).

Using passport number 725919 issued on the 18th of July 1966 (his first passport) Barrie boarded the boat, along with the other fourteen selected young men and coaches. Each one of them knowing just what they were up against, for, except for pro's like Tommy Simpson (road) and Reg Harris (track) fleetingly bucking the trend, Britain had faired badly when it came to success abroad. In a time long before lottery funding, riders had to literally use what they could get hold of as they made their way abroad. In many ways the British were still in the dark ages, whereas on the Continent, cycling was seen as something totally different, almost like that of a religion. Its top stars earning thousands and leading the life styles to match. This dominance was reflected in the Classics and the Grand Tours as the Belgians, French and Italians came out on top…not to mention the Dutch, whose country they were now entering. Quite frankly, the Great Britain team didn't stand a chance. However, they were there for the experience, it was good grounding, although, what happened next would shock them all.

Barrie was in Holland, we were in England (and as far as I know) without a phone. So, we had no idea of the heroics he was achieving. On his return home though, the press cuttings left us in no doubt.

"BARRIE ELSON LANDS BIG DUTCH PRIZES"

"TOP AWARD FOR BARRY ELSON"

38

Winning four disciplines out right, as well as the Green jersey for the title overall, Barrie was totally festooned with cups and medals as well as a bike and a watch as he made his way back to England. He had led the way on points by the end of the first day and held on right the way through to the end, scoring a magnificent win. It was truly an amazing performance. A few outstanding senior's had over the years done their country proud, and yet, here was Barrie, proving to be the first schoolboy rider to do such a thing. In the time trials, circuit and cyclo-cross races he had totally dominated, as he put his growing talent and adaptability to the fore. Why, the inhabitants of West Brabant would take him to their hearts, as never before had they seen a British rider perform like this. To finish things off, Great Britain took the Team Award as well.

If Barrie was now a Champion, then he was still a very modest one. A fact he demonstrated when he got home.

In the early hours of a Saturday morning, on arriving at Coventry train station, he would undertake the seven mile ride home with some of his bootie, before making his way back to the station to pick up the bike he had won. Whilst on arriving home for a second time (having pushed the bike alongside him) he would make himself some bacon and eggs before retiring to his bed.

Later that morning, the first the family knew of his success, was when they made their way downstairs only to discover the awards strewn across a dining room table. This was just the start though, for as word spread, it wasn't long before the local press were in the house, taking pictures of the family. Barrie, resplendent in his Green jersey, bike in hand, his Mother grinning from ear to ear holding a bouquet, his Dad (having just finished a Saturday morning shift) is trying to take it all in. Younger brother Greg, looking very adroit (if that were possible at the age of ten) and then there was me, the three year old little urchin, just getting in the way as usual (Barrie's younger sister Mandy, who was twelve at the time, wasn't there).

I'm looking at the picture now as I write. There's Mum looking all knowingly at her husband, as if to say, "We've done it!" Barrie is looking at his Dad, a look that says, are you proud of me now? Why, there was no question of that, for his son, at such a young age, was starting to totally dominate, but, he had only just begun.

NB: After Barrie's death, the family would keep hold of his GB jersey. Those were the days when it consisted of a blue body and red short sleeves (by far the best design ever as far as I'm concerned). Long before I took up cycle racing seriously, at the age of fifteen, I would allow myself to wear it on my somewhat infrequent sorties on a bike. As it was, I quite suited the colour blue, however, and much more importantly, I was close to Barrie. For he'd worn the jersey, had been victorious in it. While now, it was just me and him, I liked it that way.

'CYCLING' magazine Cyclist of the month
July 1966: Barrie Elson.

Never mind England winning the World Cup and the glory of the European victory, Barrie would receive a further honour just a few weeks later, when he was awarded the 'Cyclist of the Month' award by the 'Cycling' magazine.

The award was in its first year (the great John Atkins winning the inaugural prize in the January) and was seen as a great plaudit. But, for a mere fourteen year old schoolboy to win it, well, it was unheard of, and since. Although it was proof that Barrie was really starting to make his mark and with the new 1966/67 cyclo-cross season on the horizon, who knew what he could achieve next.

NB: Scouring through his diaries, and on a completely different matter, I noted that on the 14/7/66 (the week before he went to Holland) he would ride a four up ten mile team time trail (I'm not sure that would be allowed in a club event today). The members of the team were: "Pinder, (Ray) Ross, Mick (Blackwell) and Bas" (this was how Barrie liked to be known). They finished in a time of twenty four minutes and ten seconds.

CHAPTER NINE

Cyclo-cross season: 1966/67

After his success in Holland, Barrie returned to the calmer waters of circuit races, track and time trials as he prepared for what really was important to him, cyclo-cross. The coming months would be his last competing as a schoolboy and it was so intrinsic to him. He'd shown great promise in previous seasons, but, now it was time for him to deliver. His family, along with the press, as well as most of the cycling fraternity expected no less, for it was D Day and he didn't intend to disappoint.

By now he was fifteen years of age and in his last year as a schoolboy. Gone was the frail underling as now he was developing physically, into a burgeoning young man. Probably about 5 feet 6 inches in height and still growing, he weighed in at just under nine stone (I've estimated this based on pictures of him stood next to his Mother after his championship win).

He had, also, mastered his craft. For when it came to the technicalities needed for cyclo-cross he had the lot; poise and balance, along with, an amazing centre of gravity, which would almost keep him glued to his bike. A magician when it came to bike handling, he had the professionals of the day standing back in awe, as they tried to figure out how he had traversed a particular climb, or, descended an impossible bank without falling in a heap at the bottom. Why, Barrie's bike skills even included the ability to ride backwards. Whilst balance would be put to the test when he won a free wheeling competition; Barrie managing to stay upright when all the others had fallen. Surely then, speeding around woods would hold no fear. He had a reputation; all that was left now was to prove it.

2nd October 1966, Bromsgrove Olympic: 1st

He would start the season the way he meant to carry on. Everything was now in place, time to make his own history.

9th October 1966, VC Central: 2nd
Winner: C Browning

This turned out to be a rare defeat which saw Barrie lose to Colin Browning (Barrie had a problem with his bike on the day, which stopped him in his tracks).

When it came to the bike, Barrie's complied with most of the machines of the day, although with the odd exception. As I look at the picture of Barrie on the front page of the 'Cycling' magazine, I notice his bike looks somewhat big for him (people grew into things in that decade). Plus, I see the 'do it yourself' chain guard that his Dad had manufactured, more than likely at the cost of his firm Hawker Siddely in Lutterworth.

Barrie always used a single ring. And yet, his Dad was keen to make sure that he never lost his chain and so he would fit a slightly larger outer and inner ring to guard it, this was quite an innovation in its day. Whilst when it came to me, my Dad would fit a little strip of metal between the top of the seat tube and the end of the top tube towards the saddle, which allowed me to carry my bike under arm more easily when I was jumping over logs (I never dared bunny hopping them).

Homemade chain ring apart, the bikes back then were completely different machines to what we compete on today. There were no disc brakes, carbon frames, or, gear changing facilities where you brake. Instead, they had steel frames, centre pull brakes and handlebar control (where the gear lever protruded out of the end of the handlebar hence the name), which enabled the rider to have better control on the rough stuff. (I always thought handlebar control was so technically advanced!)

23*rd* October 1966, Warwickshire Road Club: 1*st*

Winning by over two minutes, this was a stellar feat in the day, given the length of the races (twenty five minutes). Barrie was now proving unstoppable.

30*th* October 1966, Halesowen C & AC: 1*st*

Riding the famous Manor Abbey Stadium, Barrie would chalk up his third victory of the season. The course, based around the cycle track, was made to measure for Barrie. With its tricky descents through the woods, including the need to negotiate a wet muddy wooden river bridge at speed – it would suit Barrie perfectly. (A few years later, in the early seventies, I would watch a bespectacled rider try to negotiate the same bridge before jack knifing and landing head first into the water. For a few seconds the crowd found it most amusing, whilst his Dad, on finding out that the rider had lost his glasses, immediately started a whip round.)

6th November 1966, Rugby RCC: 1st

A local event (we lived about six miles from Rugby at the time) Barrie would have no doubt ridden out as part of his preparation. By now, his weekly training mileages were far exceeding the ones of 63, 64 and 65. Indeed, in the summer of 66 (according to his diary) Barrie was averaging between one hundred and twenty five miles and one hundred and fifty miles a week. Twenty five percent of which consisted of racing and so it was quality high end stuff. We were, also, living by a large area of woods, which gave the estate its name and so Barrie would utilize it any time he wanted to practice 'off' road.

19th November 1966, Velo Club Central: 1st

His Dad would be walking the course before the race as people kept coming up to him saying: "Chicken tonight then Derrick?" He wouldn't have a clue what they were talking about, until Barrie, due-lie, won the race. As guess what the first prize was? Yes, you've guessed it, chicken (I don't think it was a live one).

Such was Barrie's dominance, that he was now turning up at races where parents and schoolboys could be heard muttering, "Elson's arrived". Although, it wasn't that he was disliked, or that he bragged, indeed, you almost had to force him to talk about how he'd performed. No, it was the fact they were now racing for second place.

27th November 1966, Smirnoff Scramble
Schoolboys: 1st

This was a prestigious race on the calendar, where the organisers at the Harlow CC really pushed the boat out and tried to set the race apart. Indeed, such were their efforts it would have an almost continental feel (it was renowned for its hog roast, which satisfied the stomachs of the large crowds). In the senior ranks, they'd bring over the top continental riders of the day and challenge the likes of John Atkins and Keith Mernicle to take them on.

Once again, Barrie proved to be the winner by over two minutes. None of the other schoolboys were getting anywhere near him now and with the National Schoolboy Cyclo-Cross Championships just a week away, he was the clear favourite.

CHAPTER TEN

"ELSON'S EXPERIENCE SHOULD SEE HIM THROUGH"

This was the headline in the Daily Telegraph on the eve of the race by the late great David Saunders. Whilst the article would read as follows:

"The third annual National Schoolboys Cyclo-Cross Championship takes place tomorrow at Aldersley Stadium Wolverhampton 2.0 with 54 young men.

Enthusiasm has grown since the first championship was held in Birmingham in 1964. No longer are there riders with ordinary shorts and shoes, riding on borrowed machines, but sturdy, well equipped lads with a great deal of dedication.

The event over six miles is a hard one with six difficult laps to negotiate and comprising all the ingredients of a good cyclo-cross course. Each circuit of a mile contains rough tracks and grassland with some sharp corners.

It will be necessary to dismount at least twice on a steep bank half way round the course, and again when entering the stadium, here the riders must climb several

47

steps before taking in a half lap of the track and then resuming the harder, muddier sections.

With a national title at stake the race is bound to be keenly contested and should provide a good spectacle for the crowds. Picking a winner is difficult as the champion for the past two years is now seventeen and too old to ride this event. He is Geoff Shaw (Wolverhampton) who now moves on to the junior class, leaving the way open for several up-and-coming riders. The competitors have come from far and wide and show the importance now attached to cycling's winter sport.

Apart from the obvious Midland Counties entries, there are competitors from London, Yorkshire, Lancashire, the Home Counties and the South. All have had considerable experience this season due to the increase in schoolboy events up and down the country.

Possible winners are Barry Elson (Coventry RC) Colin Browning (VC Central) and Ray Pinder (Coventry CC). The promoting club Wolverhampton Wheelers are pinning their hopes on two lads, Paul Paddock and Stewart Humphrey.

Elson, 15 is perhaps the outstanding rider, and he has the advantage of international experience. As a member of the Great Britain youth team, he won the Dutch Tour of West Brabant last July and will need some stopping."

His Father, a rank socialist, and just as he had done with the front cover of the 'Cycling' magazine, would once again look on in amazement as he gazed at the article (in the 'Tory Graph'). As once again, his son was being lauded, however, this time by a National broadsheet.

As the piece stated, the venue for the race was Aldersley Stadium in Wolverhampton and was to take place on Sunday 4th December 1966 (it was his Dad's birthday). However, he was unable to attend, as he had to go to Anglesey that weekend as a prerequisite of his job.

It would be a bitter pill to swallow as his Father had tracked his son's progress right from the beginning. Although, this wasn't the first race he'd missed. Without his parents having a car, Barrie had long since had to rely on lifts with yet another friend as he made his way around the country. While it would be the same this time, Mick Blackwell (a team mate and indeed, a very good friend) supplying the wheels as he, also, took Barrie's Mother.

At the time, his Mum's appearances at races could have been counted on one hand (because of the transport situation rather than through a lack of interest). And yet, there she was now, dolled up to the 'nines' ready to see her son succeed.

Well, that was the plan, for illness, a mechanical or even nerves could conspire to dash a rider's hopes. Although in Barrie's case he was having none of it. He'd trained hard, practiced well and he was now in top form as it came to the Sunday. His bike (I think it was a Mercian) thanks to his Dad, was in perfect working order and he was ready to win.

What he couldn't control, however, was the weather (there had been rain and snow in the days leading up to the race). This meant the course on the day had become a quagmire, thanks also to the wheels of the earlier junior support race (Blackwell had placed 5th in that). Incorporating technical wooded sections, as well as grassed adverse cambers and using the cycle track, all in all, it would take just over five minutes per lap to complete (the race had one lap taken off it so bad were the conditions).

The Juniors had left the course in a state, but, Barrie, given his experience had at least been able to check out the lines the other competitors had taken in some of the more difficult sections. Whilst when it came to his own preparation: he had been thorough.

Giving himself at least an hour to warm up, he would ensure that he had eaten enough (he used to live on peanut butter sandwiches), although, not too close to the event. He would then partake in a number of practice laps as he made his final choices on how he would ride the course, how best to take a corner, whether to ride or run up a bank and when it came to his tyres, what was the correct pressure. Not too high to enable good grip around the corners and not too low as to make one feel you were virtually riding on a 'flat'. Tubular tyres would be his choice of the day (where the inner tube is sewn into the tyre itself) as they gave better control along with a greater rolling resistance. Preparation over, he was now ready to go!

In cold, rather dank conditions and as the riders waited for the gun to start them, the fifty six hopefuls (not sure where Saunders got "54" from) could only wonder as to what lay ahead. Barrie knew a fast start was crucial, there were large parts of the course which discouraged overtaking, and with such talent in attendance, he couldn't risk playing 'catch up'.

Looking down at his pedals one last time he would make sure his toe clips were both open (in the days before clip-less pedals it was vital to ensure that the toe clip hadn't stuck to the pedal as that meant you couldn't get your foot in properly). He would, also, ensure he was in just the right gear (too high and it encouraged stalling, too low and he would lack any drive). Finally, he made sure he could clearly see the starter as he stood there with his gun.

So, with a heart beat increasing, standing in suspended animation, waiting for the sound of the B...five, four, three, two, one, before...WAIT!

As Barrie and the other boys lined across the start, looked across the playing field towards the car park, they would see a car screeching to a halt. Bob Russell, representing Velo Club London, had got lost on his way to the course and was now pleading with the officials to let him ride. Back then, it was a much mellower time, without Commissars who you dared not upset upon pain of death. While they weren't up against any deadline (they still had about two hours of daylight) so they let Russell ride.

The decision, although charitable, now meant that an already cold group of riders, were now getting even colder, as they were forced to wait for ten minutes whilst Russell put his wheels in, pinned his number on,

51

and took part in the briefest of warm ups (that of sprinting across the field to get to the start). In 2018, gridding itself can take up to ten minutes (which in itself is ridiculous) but, in 1966, cyclists were used to lining up and then going!

With Russell (finally) on the line, the gun went, and they were off! He would make a good start, slipping in behind Pinder with Barrie in third place as they completed the opening loop.

Come the second lap and the field began to string out; while Barrie would accelerate and move into the lead before starting to pull away. By now, Pinder was in second, with Russell in third. And it would stay that way for the next two laps, Barrie maintaining a super rhythm, hoping against hope that he didn't suffer a mechanical (in those days there were no designated pits and so if a rider had trouble he'd have to hope that his helpers were close at hand with a spare machine). However, at the start of the bell lap, with Barrie still in first place, Russell would shoot past Pinder (as the 'Cycling' reported it) and begin to close the gap. Barrie (and alerted by the noise of the crowd) was aware of this and would push on. At the line, Russell had got the lead down to fifteen seconds, although it was too late. As in a time of twenty six minutes and forty seven seconds, Barrie had done it; he was the new National Champion!!!

Amongst much whooping and hollering (no doubt from his Mother) the press described Barrie as cock a hoop (I'm sure he was)! The trusted cycling journalist Stan Kite (writing the article for the 'Cycling') pronounced that Barrie would be set to challenge for the senior title in two or three years. For wow, he'd gone and done it. Performed on the day, justified all the hope and expectation. Whilst now and whatever happened, they could never take that title away from him. It would be in the record books for time immemorial. He'd achieved!

Meantime, yet more headlines followed.

"BARRIE ELSON HAS GREAT TITLE WIN"

"ELSON GETS COVETED JERSEY"

"TWO CHAMPIONS FOR ROAD CLUB" (See below.)

As come the Monday morning, this was the headline from David Saunders at the Telegraph:

"CONFIDENT ELSON COLLECTS SCHOOLBOY TITLE"

Whilst on the Thursday morning, once more his Father looked down at yet another headline in the 'Cycling' magazine.

"ANOTHER COVENTRY RC CROSS TITLE"

NB: by now his team mate John Atkins was starting to collect titles.

The headline, together with a full back page spread, also, came with a picture of his son, all muddy faced, being kissed by a proud Mum…handbag in hand. While it would be his Mother who'd have the last word on the title win, as well as, the last laugh. For given her Irish decent (she was actually born in Liverpool after the ship carrying her Mother and Father back from Canada docked), she would use her utter love of irony, as she spoke to her husband on the phone later on the Sunday.

Barrie's Dad, had no doubt been on tender hooks all day, as he waited in Wales to hear if his son had fulfilled his destiny. With Barrie having photos to attend to, interviews to do, before eventually, getting into the car and being driven back to Coventry (this was just under an hour away), as a result it was getting late when his Mum finally made the call. A trick - well and truly up her sleeve.

For some weeks leading up to the event and with the thought of the conditions in mind, Barrie had proposed a plan. He'd apply grease to the side walls of his tyres, to deflect the mud and make his passage easier. His Father (an engineer) was dead against the idea and he did his utmost to dissuade his son. For in his mind the idea was 'balmy' and he would leave no stone unturned in his effort to convince his son of the same. And yet, he knew he wouldn't be there on the day and so he wouldn't be able to stop Barrie going through with it if he wanted to.

So, as a rather tentative Father picked up the phone, the following conversation ensued:

Dad: *"Well, how did he do?"*

Mum: *"Oh, he should have listened to his Father; he kept slipping off because of the grease. He got a Bronze though."*

Dad: *"The stupid little bugger! I kept telling him and telling him, all the effort we've put in, all the time, it's an absolute bloody waste!"*

Mum: *"Well, it's a good job he did listen to you…because he won the Gold!"*

It's interesting to note that the winner of the 2018 Under 23 Mens World Championships, Rick Van Art, sprayed baking oil all over his bike before the race in an effort to deflect the mud. So perhaps Barrie was ahead of his time.

NB: I have probably read the story about the late arrival of Russell about a hundred times over the years. I even remember the first time I read about it, after having never been told by my family.

I was relatively young at the time and certainly not old enough to understand the nuances of cycle sport, although, I would feel slightly cheated, almost as if my brother had won the title by default. For what if Russell hadn't been late? What if he'd had time to warm up properly and recce the course? Well, would the result have been different? Would the history books have changed? Although, as I got older and more involved in the sport myself, I began to realise that hey, perhaps it was a two way street on the day. On the one hand

Barrie sitting on a start line, his warmed up muscles going cold...whilst there was Russell, pinging with endorphins, at the ready as he hurried towards the start line. So, perhaps it was equal and anyway, my guess is that Barrie still would have beaten him. While that's not the bias of a younger brother talking, I consider it to be a fact.

CHAPTER ELEVEN

"TOP TEN SPORTS STARS OF 1966"

Fresh from his title win, Barrie would take part in a rare double weekend the week after, again, coming out on top.

11th December 1966, Velo Club Central: 1st

11th December 1966, Velo Club Central: 1st

12th December 1966, South Penine: 1st

18th December 1966, Bradford RCC Viking Trophy: 1st

Another win in an important event, the Viking Trophy, was one of the fore runners of the National Trophy series of today (athletes from all over the country take part in a series of races on a league basis to define who is the National Trophy winner, which is seen as the second most prodigious title next to the National Championships). In those days, the schoolboys didn't race for an overall title, their first series coming about in 1983.

A rare race on a Christmas Eve...as he gave himself an early Christmas present of another win.

On the 31st December 1966 Barrie would receive yet another award when he was named as one of the top ten sports stars in Coventry (interestingly, John Atkins didn't merit a mention). Barrie took his place alongside the likes of Nigel Boocock, (speedway rider) and George Curtis (captain of Coventry City Football Club).

Jackie Birtley wrote:

"...I rate another teenager-15 years old Barry Elson, a cyclist with the Coventry Road Club.

Elson raised a stir in national cycling circles during 1966 when he led a team of British schoolboys to victory in the 10th International Tour of West Brabent, in Holland.

Only 14 at the time, Barry took the overall lead on the second day of the five-day race, and held his position until the finish.

In addition to this Green Jersey as the overall winner, Barry also won five Yellow Jerseys, several medals, a bicycle and a watch. For these outstanding performances he was elected "Cyclist of the Month"-by "Cycling", the trade paper for the sport. This was in preference to the top international stars.

Barry went on to completely dominate schoolboy cyclo-cross racing and subsequently won the British Schoolboy Cyclo-cross championship."

1st January 1967, Wolverhampton Wheelers: 1st

Start of a new year and a return to the scene of his National triumph and again, another win.

7th January 1967, Coventry CC: 1st

Another victory and this time at an event organised by our 'deadly' rivals the Coventry Cycling Club (or the C's as they were known). Growing up, I always thought the abbreviation made them sound like a bunch of wasps, while I could never understand the 'alleged' distaste the two clubs member's had for one another. Years later, it was explained to me that the Chairman of their club, had had a disagreement with the Chairman of our club and it all seemed to stem from there. Either way, it led to one of the longest running feuds on record.

8th January 1967, Viking Trophy: 2nd!
Winner: Chris Dodd

A rare loss and this time to his team mate Chris Dodd.

15th January 1967, National Junior Cyclo-Cross Championships, Featherstone: 6th
Winner: Phil Norfolk

As part of their reward for finishing in the top six in the Schoolboy National; Barrie, Chris Dodd, along with Mick Blackwell (who had chauffeured him to Wolverhampton for his title race) were due to compete in the inaugural National Junior Cyclo-Cross Championships at Featherstone (Yorkshire) representing Coventry Road Club. With it seen as such a 'jump' for schoolboys, when they hit the ranks of the seniors, then the setting up of the junior championships seemed a logical solution; its winners seen as contenders in 'cross' for years to come.

Come race day and even though Barrie was giving some of the riders nearly three years in age, he was still seen as one of the favourites to take the title. However, the course, based around a colliery (the field had to negotiate slag heaps as they made their way round) would prove to be a total non-starter for Barrie. He would finish in sixth position, Dodd in tenth place and Blackwell in thirteenth to the winner Phil Norfolk. This was good enough to give them the team title and so yet again Barrie walked away with a medal.

5th February 1967, South Western RC: 1st

On a rare excursion to the South West Barrie was back to his winning ways.

11th February 1967, Coventry Road Club: 2nd Winner: Chris Dodd

Riding in his own club's event, Barrie incurred another rare defeat; again, to his team mate Dodd (he was three months younger than Barrie and improving fast). Although, it must be pointed out that in the entire race, Chris had sat on Barrie's wheel, refusing to do any of the work, before sprinting away to take the victory at the finish. Needless to say, it was a long time before Barrie spoke to Chris again.

18th March 1967, Warwickshire Championships: 1st

Barrie would finish the season with yet another win and title. While the 1966/67 cyclo-cross season had been a master class for him. In nineteen races, he had emerged the victor on no fewer than sixteen occasions, along with achieving two second places. Barrie had now set the bench mark; he was virtually unbeatable, whilst everyone now waited in anticipation at just what he would do next.

NB: The Warwickshire Championships was the last winter cyclo-cross Barrie ever road.

CHAPTER TWELVE

"ELSON'S TITLE TREBLE"

With the cyclo-cross season still fresh in his legs, Barrie now turned his hand back to the road and track. He rode a two up 'twenty five' with his Dad in the April. It is noticeable that he was still calling him Daddy in his racing diary (bearing in mind he was fifteen now, while his Mother's Irish up bringing possibly stipulated this).

Although he excelled at cyclo-cross, track and road, when it came to time trialling, Barrie's times were never that remarkable. Indeed, they could be classed as quite average. However, it was never a discipline he was overly concerned with (Barrie used the majority of races as training). Yet, in the June of that year, he won the Beacon Schoolboys Open ten mile time trial, with a time of twenty four minutes and thirty eight seconds.

Having set the record straight when it came to 'testing' he would follow it up, riding regularly on both the Butts and Salford tracks. Here, he scored numerous wins, in events ranging from the five hundred meter sprints, to the one mile scratch races. While back on the road, he bettered his Bronze of the year before by winning the Divisional Road Race Championships.

Winning at virtually any discipline of the sport he chose to partake in, Barrie would take this form in to the National Youth Week at Crystal Palace. Scheduled at the end of May once more he would come out the victor overall.

Yet more plaudits followed, and, in the July, he was again selected by Great Britain to ride the Tour of West Brabant. This time, he would be so restricted by the handicapping, that he'd only manage sixth place overall (still pretty good given the number of boys in the field). However, what must be noted though, is there might have been a love interest.

You know, I'd never considered it before. Indeed, it wasn't something the family had ever talked about. But then, Barrie had only just reached his sixteenth birthday, so why would they?

It came to light as I was going through some old photograph albums with my sister Mandy and brother Greg. Mandy would show me a picture of a rather attractive girl sat next to her (my sister was good looking also), while on her visit to the Tour of West Brabant the year after our brother's death. As she went on to explain that this had been Barrie's girlfriend.

Girlfriend? While immediately I found myself feeling drawn to her, close some how, for I just wanted to say, "Hi, welcome to the family, thank you for liking my brother"; although, of course this wouldn't have been possible given the fact that by now she'd have been in her late sixties. Also, when my sister had said girlfriend, did she mean in the 'literal' sense. The fact was, I didn't really want to know, and I certainly didn't ask her, for something inside me didn't want to shatter the illusion.

NB: Regarding partners, and this was something I'd thought about over the years (if, however, from a rather off field perspective). Although, let's just say if Barrie had of lived, then who would he have dated and eventually married. Or rather, who missed out on marrying Barrie and possibly starting a family with him? Of course, none of this may have occurred, but, I'm sure that it would have. No, the fact remained, or as good as, that someone else in this world had a completely different life because of Barrie's death, whilst at the same time, children were probably never conceived. Of course, you could say that about every birth, death or marriage…and yet, in this case, it could be linked to a tragedy.

CHAPTER THIRTEEN

"BARRIE – LOSS TO CYCLING AND COVENTRY"

24th August 1967, Club Ten Mile Time Trial

It was now August and Barrie's birthday had come and gone. He was sixteen with the world of cycling at his feet. Yet, despite the magnitude of his success, wining in Europe and right across the UK, he was quite happy to ride the training event with the rest of his club mates. He would finish in a time of twenty five minutes and seventeen seconds; the event was won by his team mate Pete Morgan.

This was the last time Barrie ever competed in a cycle race.

"MYSTERY OF CYCLE STARS DEATH CRASH"

Tuesday 29th August 1967

That morning, Barrie got up and went to work like he always did, cycling to Jones Benfield Construction Ltd in Kenilworth, where he earned the princely sum of four pounds fifteen shilling and four d a week. While he was no doubt looking forward to seeing his cycling mates that night, as they embarked on their twice weekly 'burn up'.

Barrie was fully established in the world of cycling now. He held titles at many disciplines and he was on the brink of something big...really big. On arrival home he would take his place at the dinner table, to talk over the day's events with his Mum and Dad (usually sport and politics) whilst trying to deflect the attentions of his irksome, sickly little brother (I literally was sick and had been in hospital on numerous occasions). As once his tea had gone down, he would quickly change into his track suit and was ready for the off.

You know, over the years, I've often stopped and thought, what if. For if only Barrie had taken the time to put one more pound of air in his tyres, or, if he'd just stopped to tie a shoelace up (cycling shoes were laced in those days). Then again, it could have been a case of if only he'd ate his sausages or chips faster that night (Barrie was unusual in his eating habits, in as much as he would eat everything in order i.e. chips, followed by sausages followed by egg). Although, the fact was, I was just clutching at straws, desperate for anything that would have stopped him being there at that precise moment. For given a split second either way, he wouldn't have been and the entire history of our family would have been different.

Of course, the same could be said for the van driver. What had influenced him being there at that moment, more to the point, why was he driving like such a bloody idiot in the first place? This was never proven.

66

7.15pm: the junction of St James Lane and London Road.

Previously, I'd only ever allowed myself to listen to the theories concerning Barrie's death. Sure, there were newspaper articles in his scrap book that gave more details, but, somehow, I just couldn't bring myself to read them; something inside me not wanting to know the real cause of my beloved brother's demise. While, therefore, I found myself surmising over what had really happened.

What I did know was that he was trying to move right onto London Road, but, if that were the case, then surely the van that hit him (it was a 30 cwt vehicle owned by Aplins Transport Dunchurch near Rugby) would also have been coming from Barrie's right. For it was a road where it was easy to get up a good head of speed and so I presumed that Barrie had pulled out and the driver (given the speed he was doing) had not seen him. I mention speed, as this was something our Mother went on and on about until her dying day. She would repeatedly question the fact that although the driver had claimed he wasn't going fast, then how had Barrie been knocked forty yards across the road (I never found this reported anywhere, but I am not saying she was wrong).

As it was, Barrie's bike incurred little or no damage. Whilst the inquest report would go onto state that the left hand brake lever had been 'tapped' over, which in turn had turned the handlebars leaving a dent in his pump. In the cold light of day, on seeing the word 'tapped' mentioned, it makes one think that there may have been an element of bias, perhaps, a lack of knowledge when the inquest jury gave their verdict. For, if it was only a 'tap', then how did that explain the fractured skull which Barrie sustained? That aside, the bike did indeed get off lightly, Barrie suffering the damage. And yet, why didn't he suffer any other injuries, say, to his legs? Given his Mother's opinion, along with the seriousness of his head injuries, we can only suspect, but we'll never know as no witnesses came forward (which again was unusual given the area and the time of night).

Nevertheless, that still left the 'actual' direction the van was travelling in. For instead of coming from the right (as I had first suspected), plus, given the fact that Barrie could have been hidden by the surrounding houses (as a result he may have been more susceptible when it came to a impact), what I couldn't accept was what I read next, which stated that the van had in fact been turning right into St James Lane.

Over the years, and partly because I had to negotiate the junction everyday on my way to school, I had had the opportunity to assess exactly where Barrie and the van driver were at the point of impact. However, the fact of the matter was, it just didn't make sense. For given the fact that the driver was turning right, then this in turn would have given him a panoramic view of what was happening in front of him. Barrie, therefore, would have been visible. So, what the hell did happen that night to cause Barrie's death? Like I say, I've traversed the same junction many times, each of which, I've never been able to do so without thinking of my brother. While as an experienced driver myself now, then there can be only one conclusion.

Barrie would have looked where he was going, he wasn't a fool. Barrie was an experienced cyclist and he would have been able to judge what was in front of him and the danger(s) it imposed. Except, let's just say, that the van driver was speeding. Barrie would have looked left before making the decision to pull out. However, if the van driver was going that fast, then perhaps in that split second, he wasn't in Barrie's peripheral vision. Then, let's look at the evidence concerning the damage to his bike and the fact that his legs were unhurt. Well, all that can suggest is that the van hit Barrie right at the front of his bike, which in turn swung the handlebars round and dented the pump. This would have required some force! But the jury quoted the word 'tapped' when it came to the front left hand brake leaver. So, that didn't explain (and bearing in mind Barrie had both arms on the handle bars) how such an alleged minor force could then do what it did. Not only that, the van's point of impact on Barrie's bike must have been quite high, because, there was no mention of damage to any of the wheels. So, it looks like the handlebars took the impact.

So, in the cold light of day, this is what I think happened: I believe Barrie couldn't see the van as he pulled out right, rather than, seeing the van and taking a chance. I think if that had been the case, then the van would have hit the bike more towards the centre and the back. Again, I come back to the part of the bike the van

69

hit, as this would suggest Barrie would have had every chance to avoid the crash by simply braking. While basically, I think the van driver himself misjudged just how fast Barrie could be and therefore hit him, rather than just missing him. Once more, coming back to the velocity of the impact, it would smash one of the vans lights out. However, that then leaves Barrie, as I never read anywhere that the impact had caused him to go over the van. No, for given its high frontal area, the speed it was going, I believe it made contact with Barrie's bike before throwing him in to the air and his eventual death.

At the time, the driver was adamant that he wasn't speeding and with no witnesses it was always going to be difficult to prove otherwise. Whilst the jury would conclude that there could have been better road marking (although I fail to see what they meant by this) and furthermore, that the junction was dangerous (although I think the same could be said of any junction if the rules of the Highway Code are not adhered too). Not long after the incident, traffic lights would be erected to stop that type of accident ever happening again. Although, unfortunately, it was too late, for Barrie was already gone.

There were no mobile phones in those days and so I'm not even sure who called the ambulance (I think the call may have been made from a nearby fish and chip shop). As on arrival, Barrie would be rushed straight to the Coventry and Warwickshire hospital in a critical condition.

Later that evening on her way to work, his Mum, totally unaware of Barrie's plight would gaze at the blood and glass on the road from her motorbike as she rode past the very same junction. 'Someone's had a bad one' she thought to herself, unaware of the horror that was just about to hit her.

As it was his Dad was given the news first; the police waking him from his slumber (as he slept in a chair) before racing to the hospital to meet his wife.

As for me, my only memory is that of waiting in a cold dark hallway late at night, standing alongside Mandy and Greg, just waiting for news. The eerie silence as I looked skywards towards an older sister and brother, hoping they would make it all better, make it all go away. They couldn't. They just couldn't.

NB: It was probably only two years ago that Dad and I were sat down one day drinking our habitual cups of tea when the talk got onto Barrie. Quite understandably, Dad only talked about that night if asked and I certainly wasn't going to press him. But, suddenly, he would come out with it.

Medical science was nowhere near as advanced in 1967 as it is today. So, on being told that they could do no more for his son; he would be left holding Barrie's hand as he waited for him to die.

I was a Father myself by this time and on hearing his word's I just wanted to cry.

The photograph that inspired a book

The magnificent Charlie Craig

A mischievous child

The Tour that made a Champion!

Front cover of the 'Cycling'

British team in Holland

Press shoot

Number one

A proud Mother

National Champion

CHAPTER FOURTEEN

The news of Barrie's death soon reverberated around the cycling world. In the days before the internet many people took the time to write letters of condolence.

This is one we received from the late Keith Edwards, the President of the British Cyclo-Cross Association at the time:

30th August 1967

Dear Mr and Mrs Elson,

I was shocked to hear this morning of Barrie's untimely death. Although I only knew him slightly I was particularly impressed by his modesty despite the considerable success attained by one so young.

As a rider I regarded him of one of a handful of natural cyclo-cross riders in this country and I had hoped to see him representing Great Britain at senior level within the next two years.

Your loss is a great one but take some consolation from the knowledge that in his short life Barrie achieved more than most men in a normal lifetime and this reflects great credit on both of you.

Yours sincerely

Keith Edwards

The press also paid their respects:

Charles Porter: Coventry Evening Telegragh

"BARRIE LOSS TO CYCLING AND COVENTRY"

Riding a bicycle was as natural to Barrie Elson as was walking. His death in a road accident this week is a tragedy for the sport of cycling nationally as well as locally.

Amateur cycling in Britain has probably never suffered a loss as being deprived of the present and future brilliance of Barrie.

Reporting on a track meeting earlier this year I used the phrase: 'Schoolboys performing like old masters...' Barrie Elson was one of the boys to whom I referred.

Apart from his outstanding ability, he had two other qualities without which a sportsman is never complete – complete lack of conceit and an inexhaustible supply of good humour.

In the meantime, his Mother and Father had a funeral to organize (unfortunately, I was thought too young to attend). The service took place at St Margaret's Church in Wolston, on Tuesday 5th September 1967.

Five hundred mourners attended the service, the police having to control the traffic. John Atkins and Mick Ives were among the pall bearers. Barrie would be buried in his National Championship jersey.

As I write this book, I'm looking at some slides of the grave, bedecked as it is with wreath after wreath. It seems a bright warm autumnal day, a day Barrie would have taken advantage of to go out on his bike.

The hole Barrie's death left in the hearts of the Elson family was unimaginable, with some members perhaps never quite recovering. So much to live for, but now, he was gone.

NB: Perhaps the most poignant part of the whole horrendous episode was the writing that I found at the end of Barrie's racing log book. His painstaking record keeping had chronicled all of his competitive races as a schoolboy, from the early days as a fourteen year old, right up to present day. His National title win, noted under the heading of 'me', whilst he'd written a greatly enlarged 1st.

However, Barrie was obviously planning for the future, as a few pages on from the above, was the word "JUNIOR" 1967/8/9 with the headings date, name of event, winner, and finally "my placing" (he obviously didn't want to put 'me' anymore).

Barrie never got to ride those races and so underneath his Mother wrote this:

"Barrie died as the result of a road accident August 29th 1967

You never got the chance to do your Junior rides
But we know you would have won
Not one day will we forget you, in our hearts you will be always there."

CHAPTER FIFTEEN

THE AFTERMATH

A few weeks later, when Dad was riding on his bike with Barrie's younger brother Greg, our Father would literally want to kill a motorist after he nearly took his son off the road.

Greg was four years younger than Barrie and would be next in the production line achieving some notable victories. A Midland Champion, he'd come seventh in the Schoolboy Championships at Southampton in 1970. Only just fifteen, he would be severely hampered in the race by a broken gear cable, which meant he was stuck in a low sprocket. Whilst he would miss out on potential glory the next year at Sutton Coldfield due to turning sixteen just before the Championships (unlike today, when your age and consequent eligibility to ride is taken at the start of the season, then, it was a case of you had to be under sixteen on the day of the race). I cannot be certain, but I think the loss of a potential title win proved the un-doing of Greg and he'd disappear from the sport soon after.

Our sister Mandy also tried out cycle racing, competing in the odd time trial. Despite this, her interests lay elsewhere. She would, however, do her brother's memory proud, when she represented the family as a guest of the British team at the 1968 edition of the Tour of West Brabant.

Uncertain as to how she'd be received, the reception she enjoyed would overwhelm her, whilst the warmth was tangible as all around people conveyed stories of just how good Barrie had been. Why, as she passed by people's houses, she'd see pictures of her brother displayed in windows, which brought tears to her eyes.

So, that would just leave me. I'd ride some little boy's races in the very early seventies, even scoring some wins. However, just like Mandy and Greg had done, I would leave the sport, returning to racing on the eve of my fifteenth birthday. By now, I'd missed out on the apprenticeship that Barrie and Greg had served; therefore, I'd suffer the many losses they had had to endure when they first began.

Although after a few seasons, my form would improve, and the wins followed. I was nineteen now and I could go to most races and expect a top six finish (that was never seen as good enough by my Father). Yet, I was never going to win a National title, or, earn a living from the sport. So, in that moment, I decided to walk away (once again) and devote all the hours (twelve a week) I was giving to training over to studying.

And yet, as the years went by, I needed to scratch that itch. For I'd finished the studying, started a business, become a Father to a beautiful baby girl; so that just left world domination in the world of cyclo-cross.

I would come back as a veteran this time. After weeks of hard training (three hundred miles a week) I was sure I would soon be knocking the spots off my inferior rivals. As it was, it would be me who would be left floundering, as my body suddenly informed a mind that there was no way you could neglect it for twenty years and expect it to perform again (bugger).

Undeterred, I would carry on and one season became two. I started training with the National Coach Martin Eadon (himself a former National Champion), who'd put me through the most tortuous of training regimes. As slowly, very surely, it began to work! I would eventually score a win at Shipston-on-Sour, almost riding myself into the ground to finally prove myself once again. The acid test, however, was whether I could do it at a National level.

One bright autumnal morning I lined up with the rest of the field at a National Trophy event in Cheltenham. In previous events of the same stature, I'd found myself making up the numbers, as despite the training, my body wasn't quite ready to perform. Although, this time, it was different.

As the gun sounded, I made my way off in about 40th position (this was due to my low gridding), and yet, as the race progressed, instead of going backwards, I started scything my way through the field. For gone was the lactic acid in my legs, the breathlessness of my lungs, that had so held me back before, as now I started to make my way up towards the front.

I could literally feel the ease, as one by one, I overtook the next competitor. By the start of the third lap, I could see the tenth placed rider in front of me, as he fought to stay in contention with the next group of riders just ahead of him.

I was doing it, I was literally doing it! I was flying; there was nothing that could hold me back. After all the years of living in the shadows and then...suddenly, the lights went out.

I woke later, in Cheltenham General Hospital, surrounded by my wife, daughter and brother Greg, he had stopped to help me as soon as he saw the accident (Greg had made a brief comeback to the sport and was riding that day). It appeared I had ridden down a gulley when attempting to avoid some course marking that had come loose in the wind. While somehow, unlike Barrie, I was okay, or at least I thought I was. It would turn out that I had broken my back and although I'd recover and go on to compete again, the fact was: I would never be the same rider.

NB: When I say I raced again, this was after much deliberation and again after hour upon hour of training. My last training ride (on the eve of my first race back) saw me partake in a sixty mile round trip to Stratford. On my journey home, to alleviate the boredom, I put my head down and dreamt that I was leading a classic with only a few kilometres to go.

Once again, I would wake up in a hospital bed, after going into the back of a car which had stopped on a country lane as the driver made a phone call. The hospital this time though was the Coventry and Warwickshire, the same one Barrie had been rushed to

88

all those years ago. A relieved wife by my bedside once more, I just laid there and cried. "Why do I keep on living?" I would exclaim "When Barrie had to die".

For the last five years, I have been paid to commentate on cycle racing. As I've had the privilege to interview several big names such as Magnus Backstedt and Dame Sarah Storey, however, the rider I've always wanted to commentate on and subsequently interview is Tom Pidcock. An immense talent, who seems to be able to win at anything he chooses to (remind you of anyone at all?).

I did at least, have the pleasure of shaking Tom's hand as he came off the podium after his Under 23 National Cyclo-Cross title win at Hetton Lyons in 2018. He had ridden superbly to take the title, but, what impressed me most was the handshake. It was firm, whilst he looked directly into my eyes. That to me equalled sincerity, a quality that will see him go very far in life, never mind cycling.

At the Junior World Championships in Luxemborg in 2017, he would lead the Great Britain team to a Gold, Silver and Bronze as he was followed in by Dan Tulett and Ben Turner. Barrie would never have dreamed that a GB team could achieve such success, as they dominated the race from start to finish.

However, it's not only the young men who are proving successful. Evie Richards now has two Under 23 Women's World Championship titles to her credit. I would interview her at the 2017 West Midlands Championships, where she was making a comeback after injury. Not surprisingly, she would go on and win that day, but far more importantly, she was just a lovely individual.

So, the future is bright when it comes to the sport of cyclo-cross in this country, as our star performers begin to make it big in Europe. British cycle racing has been dragged kicking and screaming in to the big league thanks to the likes of the Lottery Funding and Team Sky. While thankfully, cyclo-cross has now joined the party and with the grass roots so strong (as I said, the local leagues have upwards of five hundred people registered) there is no saying where it may end up.

CHAPTER SIXTEEN

When it came to the future, then there's no telling just what Barrie would have achieved if he'd have lived. For he had the lot, he quite literally oozed talent.

Meanwhile, there are few bench marks. Most of the riders Barrie rode against gave the sport up as they got older and discovered girls, drink, study and work as they realised something had to give - it was usually cycling. However, there was one rider who carried on. His natural ability, perhaps deeming it was too important to waste on a night out, or, a broken heart of an unrequited love, his name, Chris Dodd (the rider suffering on Barrie's wheel in the photograph).

Throughout Barrie's amazing last season at 'cross' (66/67), Chris had had to play second fiddle, but, there was no doubt he was good. After Barrie's death, Chris would be prevented from winning a Schoolboy title in his own right, as he turned sixteen a few weeks before the 1967 Championships at Oldbury. He would, also, go on to win two Junior titles at Denton (1968) and Hessle (1969), a Stronglight Cotterless Chainset forming part of the winning. Two Amateur Championships followed at Leeds (1972) and Sutton Coldfield (1973), as in those days the Amateur race was run in conjunction with the Professionals with separate Gold, Silver and Bronze Medals being given out.

The crowning glory for Chris though would come at the Amateur World Championships in Appledorn

Holland in 1971. Here, he would finish an incredible sixth. This was even more remarkable as in those days, as mentioned previously and bar the odd exception, most British competitors were no more than bit part players to their more accomplished European rivals. Why, instead of victories, we'd read of yet another excuse concerning the weather, or, the fact one of our team had suffered an 'itchy' finger. I digress, as the fact was, we weren't good enough. However, on that day, Chris proved otherwise.

Chris would go on to ride as a professional; his team Bantel included the great sprinter Sid Barras and Hugh Porter (the four times World Professional Pursuit Champion).

So, Chris was good, world class in fact! Yet Barrie could beat him, so, what would have happened? I've thought long and hard about writing this piece, as the last thing I wanted to do was appear to besmirch Chris's achievements as they were outstanding. On the other hand, it still leaves the question. Of course, Chris could have ended up beating Barrie, or, perhaps, Barrie might have married his 'girlfriend' from Holland and ended up as a hairdresser in the Outer Hebrides! Unfortunately, we'll never know. Although, my guess would be that Barrie would have been up there, challenging and eventually winning. Moreover, the record books would have been different.

I never really knew Chris when he was racing against my brother (I was under five at the time). So, the first time I encountered him was at a cyclo-cross in Rugby when my own fledgling career was starting out

(1980). He was still a top rider at the time and I've got a picture of him lapping me as he went on to win the race. Our paths would cross again a few weeks later, when he organised some training weekends, instructing us in every aspect of cyclo-cross. I'd impress him when it came to the one hundred metre sprints from a standing start that we did in preparation for the starts in the races. One of the riders there was Lance Ravenhill; he was older than me and the reigning Coventry Divisional Sprint Champion (he would also win several Veteran titles at cyclo-cross). Although on the day, he could get nowhere near me (nor could the others) when it came to the sprints, causing him to say, "Blimey, he doesn't even shave his legs!" after he was dealt, yet another drubbing!

Yet, looking back and even though Chris was intrinsic when it came to my history, we never spoke, or, should I say, we never spoke about Barrie. I was eighteen at the time and my head was probably in a different place; although, in a way, I never really connected Chris with him anyway. Of course, if I met Chris now (I haven't seen him for the best part of thirty years) I'd quiz him relentlessly about their relationship. Indeed, I had thought about doing so as part of my research for this book, but, I wasn't convinced I would get much insight. My experience of asking questions to people who knew Barrie was normally "he was class". I needed to know more.

Going back to the last time I had any contact with Chris it was 1989, after he'd had a short absence from the sport. He was making a comeback as a veteran (in those days it was for riders over thirty five, Chris was thirty eight) with the soul aim of winning the veteran category in the National Championships held in Bedale, Yorkshire.

We seemed closer than we had done at the training sessions. I was older for one and more rounded as an individual (some might have argued otherwise). Yet, we still didn't mention Barrie. It mattered little though, as now I was in his corner, vying for him to win. For Chris was from the class of 66 and if he could win, then he was also winning for Barrie.

We travelled to the race by coach, along with other locals from the Coventry area. I still recall Mick Ives (riding for the Coventry Olympic and the eventual winner) calmly devouring a pot noodle in the car park as we got off the coach, with the race no more than a few hours away; I'd think to myself, "how an earth is he going to digest that?" He did though, whilst Chris would finish well back in about sixteenth place. It sure broke my heart on the day, as I'd covered virtually every blade of grass shouting him on, encouraging him, but, to no avail. Of course, for Chris to have won that day would have taken some doing. Like I say, he'd been away from the sport for some time and was relying on the recent training regime he'd undertaken along with his vast knowledge of 'cross'. However, it wasn't good enough.

Chris would go on to ride one more season, this time it included the 1990 Championships in Birmingham. The event, run in the shadow of Spaghetti junction, once

94

more saw Chris 'bomb' as Lance Ravenhill took the title.

This proved to be a devastating blow to him. Why, he'd dominated as a junior and senior, taking many titles. Hence, he thought he would win the Veteran title also. Sadly, it was not to be, and Chris never competed in cycling again.

NB: At one point in his career Chris held both the junior cyclo-cross and road titles.

CHAPTER SEVENTEEN

So, the record books, would they have changed? Perhaps the rider who'd have been most affected by this was the legend John Atkins. Whilst again, I am not seeking to belittle John, for like I say, he was a legend.

Of course, today, you only have to be able to win an event, without falling off, to start being recognised as such (a legend). Nonetheless (and just like the word depressed, is banded about if you have a bad hair day), it is a word that is far too common place these days. On the other hand, in John's case, it was true. Amassing thirteen National Cyclo-Cross senior titles, as well as achieving a 5th place finish in the Amateur Worlds in Luxemborg in 1969 (finishing only fourteen seconds behind the winner, still the best senior placing we have ever achieved) he was something special.

For just like Barrie, John had an amazing bike handling ability, as well as ring craft, which he'd put to good use when the international stars of the day visited our shores. In lesser events, he would be happy to race round in the pack, breaking away towards the end and winning by a few seconds (John would often accomplish this, by say running up a bank that was thought un-rideable, before riding up it on the last lap and getting away, such was his cunning).

However, when the likes of the Belgian World Champion Vermiere came across and the hammer went down, John would respond to the pace and go with them

(John recording a famous victory at Manor Abbey Stadium in Halesowen in the early Seventies). A legend and my hero, from the first time I saw him ride at the scene of Barrie's title win at Aldersley Stadium in 1971; as John came out the woods leading a four man pack which included Chris Dodd, Eric Stone and Vic Barnett. For John had everything, a flare, glamour along with the Marsh and Baxters sponsored car that they provided him with and which I thought so cool at the time.

Such was John's fame in the day that he was the star in a Marathon (Snickers) advert, as it extolled the virtues of the chocolate bar when it came to helping athletic performance (I suppose it might have helped). Why, as a kid, I was in no doubt and I'd collect my half a crown of pocket money from my Dad on a Thursday (Dad's pay day) before racing up to the paper shop at the top of our road on my bike. The return trip after devouring the said bar being completed in record time (EPO, who needed it)!

Moving on to the present day, I would find myself commentating at our club's Boxing Day cyclo-cross event at Kenilworth Common in Warwickshire (the oldest cyclo-cross on the calendar, dating back to the 50s). Part of the legend of the race (and this is a Father's recollection we are talking about) is that Chris Dodd would pass John in mid air one year, when negotiating the turrets (almost vertical long descents through the woods), before going onto win.

John had long since given up racing by now (except for when he had made a comeback in the over 50's category in 2001 losing out to Chris Gooch) and was happy to talk as I called him over. I could feel a tangible hush in the crowd as I prepared to interview him. After all, this was John Atkins. Meanwhile, we'd talk for about ten minutes about his career. As throughout the entire exchange, I would play the part of the diligent interviewer, taking the conversation this way and that, whilst inside, I was the little boy once again, talking to my hero Marathon bar in hand.

Although, the question remains, would Barrie have made any difference to John's illustrious career? You know, I'm going to duck out on this one, for how can we ever truly know? Sure, Chris would push John all the way when he hit the senior ranks. However, it would be John who would score the baulk of the victories. So, would Barrie have ended up somewhere in the middle? You know, the middle was never a place my brother was comfortable in, for he preferred to be first, pure and simple, with a DNA that deemed he just had to win. So, I will leave the jury out on this one.

NB: One thing Barrie would never have tolerated as he made his way up the ranks was the drug culture that was prevalent on the European scene. For long before the Festina affair and Armstrong, the pros abroad had become used to taking their little helpers. For he'd already mourned the loss of his hero Simpson when amphetamines had made his body try and do something it couldn't. However, if Barrie had thought that such practices were reserved for the tour riders of the day, he was wrong. As it was, he wouldn't live to see the

98

jailing of the seven times World Professional Champion Eric De Vlaeminck of Belgium just twelve months after his title win at Crystal Palace in 1973. (My Dad and I were officials on the day and our job was to clean the winner down and present him too the press...as it turned out we would not get near him!) Either way, Barrie would have hated it.

CHAPTER EIGHTEEN

The Barrie Elson Memorial Trophy Race

By now, I'd had Barrie's memorabilia box, scrapbook and results log book, as well as his picture on my wall for what seemed like forever. However, apart from the odd exception, when I might have got it all out to show off to some unsuspecting individual (as I attempted to eulogize as to just how good he was) the fact remained, his memory was fading. Barrie had been dead for forty years, so why would he be remembered? I needed to sort it.

I was still married at the time. Whilst my wife raised no objection to my idea of sponsoring a schoolboy cyclo-cross race in Barrie's memory, with a trophy and a winner's prize of one hundred pounds (this made it the biggest prize in schoolboy racing). As a result, I would speak to the organizer (Andy Jones) of the Wolverhampton Wheelers cyclo-cross event, whose event was at Aldersley Stadium. The scene of Barrie's title triumph as I felt it only right we held it where his dream had been realised.

Just like in 1966, it was a dank, cold day as I trudged across the car park towards the course. I was rather laden down, for as well as the Barrie Elson Memorial

Trophy (a shield), I also had the photograph that had been on my wall, along with a flip chart stand. I had spent days during the previous week going through all of Barrie's racing pictures and newspaper headlines as I sought to create a montage of success in his memory (hence the flip chart). I, also, had a list documenting Barrie's palmarès as my aim was to have it all in full view by the course, so people could see exactly what he'd achieved.

NATIONAL SCHOOLBOY CYCLO-CROSS CHAMPION

WINNER OF THE TOUR OF WEST BRABANT

WINNER OF THE NATIONAL JUNIOR TEAM AWARD with Chris Dodd and Mick Blackwell.

CYCLING WEEKLY'S CYCLIST OF THE MONTH

WINNER OF THE NATIONAL YOUTH WEEK

WARWICKSHIRE CYCLO-CROSS CHAMPION

COVENTRY DIVISIONAL ROAD RACE CHAMPION

NOMINATED ONE OF THE TOP TEN SPORTS STARS IN COVENTRY

NB: At the time I forgot to mention the dates.

When it came to the photograph, I'd thought long and hard about taking it. After all, it was a private possession to our family. However, I reasoned that if we were to have a race in Barrie's name, then the public had a right too see what he looked like. More importantly (as far as I was concerned) I'd liberated Barrie once from a dingy wardrobe, now I was taking him back to where he truly belonged.

Throughout the day, I would sneak a peek towards where I had stationed my tribute, feeling a sense of butterflies in my stomach every time someone stood to observe it. Barrie had occupied a part of my heart and a compartment in my brain all my life under the heading 'special'. While now I was downloading it, as the imaginary became physical. Once more I wanted to cry.

The commentator for the event (Robyn Kyte) remembered Barrie. He'd raced against him in the National he'd won. Indeed, it was all very apt, the past, meeting the present; all the pieces coming together.

Before the race, I was called to the start line to say a few words. I hadn't expected to be asked and I had nothing prepared to say. So, I just stood there, a hundred eager eyes looking at me. I told them briefly about Barrie, his title win and ultimate passing. It all seemed so surreal. My mind began to race between a thousand circumstances; the hallway, the fables, the pictures, the medals and the cupboard. Now, Barrie was free, free for me to tell the racers of the day. For he wasn't 'gone' any more, he was no longer a memory. He was in the here and now, he was present.

I had no real idea of where the start line had been situated all those years ago in December 66, it could have been anywhere. Although I chose for it to be where we were stood that day and as I looked at a Halesowen rider I could just see Barrie tucked in beside him, his eyes focused just ready for the gun!

Joshua Papworth would be the first winner. My daughter Aimear (who was just four years old) would present the prize. It was a great day, a memorable one in fact. Barrie had been put back on the stage, people had spoken about him again, and elder cyclists had even recognised him. Mission accomplished! As, slowly, very surely, I hoped that his name would now start to resonate.

Ten years on, the event has gone from strength to strength, with a whole cast of young stars winning his trophy (some winning National Champions in their own right). As that's what I always wanted, the best prize, for the best rider, just like Barrie had been.

Harry Yates of Hargrove Cycles would win it one year. In another book I'd written about my own childhood I'd called Barrie, Harry, as I attempted to write in pseudonym. Why Harry even looked like him.

In 2017, to commemorate the 50th year of Barrie's passing, I made a request to the sports ruling body (British Cycling) to see if they would let me present the award to that year's National Schoolboy Champion at Bradford. Unfortunately, I never heard back from them.

Whilst in 2016, I would give the award to the winner of the under 12s race (the racing in this category that season had been so good I thought it only fair). Jude De Toit took the win. While later he beat me in a mini bike challenge, so I guess he deserved the money!

The list of winners:

JOSHUA PAPWORTH
LUKE GREVILL MELLOR
JOE FOX
JACK RAVENSCROFT
EWAN GREVILL MELLOR
LOUIS KILWORTH
HARRY YATES
JUDE de TOIT
LEWIS ASKEY

NB: It wouldn't only be me who honoured Barrie's name. To a lesser extent, the organisers of the National Youth week at Crystal Palace would also have a special trophy made. Whilst his team, the Coventry Road Club, commissioned a cup which they presented to the winner of a designated schoolboy cyclo-cross. I would win it one year

BREAKING NEWS: As the book goes to print, Lewis Askey has won the Junior Paris Roubaix.

CHAPTER NINETEEN

As I lay in my bed, amidst damp conditions, I imagine yet another piece of wall paper pealing from the wall, another curtain exaggerating its drape, unable as it is to support the weight. What have I done? More to point: why did I choose this place? Cost, dear boy, cost. Twenty pounds bed and breakfast all in, bargain!

I should have known better when Mrs Shini (she was a Korean lady) showed me round the day before. But you see I was desperate, I'd left my booking far too late and now all the good rooms in town had gone. So, I was left with this one. I cared not, as I needed some semblance of belonging in my world. I'd recently split from my wife and had lost a lot of contact with my daughter as a result. Now I needed the family of 'cross' like I'd never needed it before. Money was tight and so beggars couldn't be choosers.

Oh, how I begged after the first races on the Saturday, as I sought refuge on the bedroom floor of a cycling buddy, in his plush hotel bedroom, just so I could avoid going back 'there'. It was to no avail. However, at least now, I'd be able to leave soon, back to the races. Although, before I can go, I have a duty to carry out.

Fried bread, a must in the Elson household, and yet Mrs Shini had no idea how to cook it. It is quite simple;

105

you leave it until the very end, when all the bacon, tomatoes and sausages are done, but not forgetting the egg. For the egg is important, vital in fact, as the egg acts as the weight on top of bread, as on turning the heat up, it helps enhance the frying…before, job done! Not forgetting to do the other side as well of course.

Why Mrs Shini, despite appearing enthusiastic (she was in fact a lovely woman, just a shame about her décor), would fail miserably! I cared not, as I was about to escape!

So keen was I to vacate the digs from hell that I must have been one of the first people to arrive at the course for the under 23, Ladies and Senior events. Fact was though, I was bored. However, as I perused the signing on quarters and its rather ornate surrounding, I would come across a book that had recently been published, 'Blood Sweat and Gears' by Ken and Maureen Nichols which chronicled the history of cyclo-cross in this country from the nineteen fifties.

Its material (most likely) taken from the cycling journals of the day was a fascinating piece of script. As it detailed every season and star performance; almost like a pen joining up the memories inside my head. Cyclo-cross had always played such a positive enjoyable part of my life and now the book was reliving it all over again.

Atkins, Mernickle, Dodd, Stone, Davies…these were just some of the names I'd write on some old dice as they now became the competitors in my own version of the National Championships. I was only about ten, and on a Monopoly board that had been converted into Sutton Park (in my mind anyway) I would use another pair of dice to take a throw and see how far each rider went. Why I would even provide my own commentary (who'd have thunk it!).

Although the book wasn't quite mimicking my somewhat crazy past (when it came to do it yourself board games), it was at least reminding me why I loved the sport so much, the camaraderie, excitement, the shear brilliance of some of the riders. Then there were the races, Sutton Park (again) 1978 where Chris Wreghitt finally ended the dominant run of John Atkins in a exciting sprint finish (I maintain to this day that John shouldn't have paused when he came out the woods onto the road section which allowed Chris to get back up to him). Roundhay Park, Leeds (1992), the World Junior Cyclo-Cross Championships as Roger Hammond enters the woods to begin the long run up, the crowd's roar like that of Elland Road (Leeds United's ground) as Allan Clarke scores yet another goal (showing my age). Finally, Sutton Park 1999, National Elite Championships (they changed its name), as Steve Knight (an amateur) does the ride of his life catching Nick Craig (a professional) right at the end.

You know, I was going great guns with the book, loving every sentence of it, that is, until I got to page eighty two.

I hadn't even thought for a moment that it would detail anything about what Barrie had done (I'm not sure why really, as he was a big enough name). Yet, there he was, as it gave details of his title win, whilst the prizes went down to 20th place. As I continued to read, I would feel myself beginning to feel quite moved (I was susceptible anyway as I was missing my daughter) before the start of another chapter on page 88 would finally prove my downfall.

"Season 67/68

In August the sport would hear of a tragic accident, which was reported in The Coventry Evening Telegraph: "Young Cycling Star Dies after a Coventry road accident. Barrie Elson, one of Britain's most promising racing cyclists died in the Coventry and Warwickshire hospital today. Barrie became Schoolboy National Champion last December. In July 1966 Barrie was acclaimed in Dutch newspapers after he won the 'Tour of West Brabant'-he was captain of the team that won the team event." The sport had therefore lost not only a present champion but also a star of the future."

As I struggled to take in the words, I just sat there sobbing, as I looked out towards a cyclo-cross course, Barrie's domain. I'd felt so damn lonely moments earlier, I was on my own and I didn't know what the future held. Reading about my brother, it would tip me over the edge, as all my psychological chickens came home to roost. I'd sat with Aimear just a few months earlier, as we'd painstakingly perused his scrapbook, while I even allowed her to write her own words in it, she was his niece after all.

108

"Dear Uncle Barrie,

45 years on and your family is looking through your things. Your little brother Adrian who is my Dad is Fifty next Thursday. Your niece, Aimear loves you and wishes that you were here. Aimear is me. I've got your scrapbook and am writing in it now. When you died, there was so many articles about you. I was born in 2003 and am 9 years old. I am writing this in the year 2012 and although you probably will not ever get to see this, just know that you are in our hearts. My Father loved you and still loves you now although he does not remember you. Last year I road the under tens in your memorial race although what I mean by last year is that I mean January. As you are probably awhere of that my Granma and your Mother died 14 years after you and was buried in the same grave. I love you and Gran and hope that one day an Elson from our Family does as well as you did. ♥

Lots of Love
Aimear

XXX ♥ "

NB: I would have the privilege of interviewing Chris Wreghitt at a race in Birmingham in 2017 as he started his come back to the sport. He had drifted away after winning five National titles and now at the age of fifty nine, he was going for another, in the over 60's.

As a boy growing up, Chris had been a bit of an enigma to me. I didn't know him personally, but, I had led him in a race at Aldersley Stadium in an ICS (International Cycle Sport) event for all of 400 yards in the early 80's after I'd jumped the start. He was also the man who had provided the downfall of my hero, whilst he didn't seem to quite have the charisma that John had provided (I was no doubt rather bias). However, the fact remained that he seemed quite a mechanical sort of rider, who'd take part in his cross country running events on a Saturday (he had been a student of Loughborough University, where running was encouraged, not least because of the exploits of another former student, Olympic 1500 metre Champion Sebastian Coe) before rocking up on a Sunday and giving the rest of the field a kicking (he would even give the riders a two minute head start in some races and still beat them).

He would do all this as he took the sport to another level, as it came face to face with 'sports science'. Although, the fact remained, that I still thought him rather aloof. Why my mind would still be firmly implanted in an age over forty years ago (I was good at that) as I plucked up the courage, to ask him to come across for a few words. As in a split second, I was the disgruntled ignorant little youth again, who knew 'stuff all' about 'cross' who was about to try and converse with a 'star' rider; who, was going to tie me in knots, whilst no doubt being grumpy, as he went about it (ah yes, I also thought he seemed grumpy as well, as I

110

perused a picture of him running up a bank in the 'Cycling' magazine all those years ago).

On the day, as he wheeled his bike towards me, I would see him stop and exchange a cursory word with Andy Jones (the organiser of Barrie's race). It was then that I saw the smile (I'd never seen him smile before), of course, I'm sure he had smiled plenty of times (five at least) and yet what that was telling me now, was that he was okay.

We would talk for at least fifteen minutes, about his amazing career; his sorties into Europe as it suddenly dawned on me what an engaging, interesting intelligent but above all level headed guy he was. You know, I think his comeback has proved to be somewhat of a culture shock to him, but I for one look forward to commentating on him in the future.

CHAPTER TWENTY

6th November 2017, Team Jewson Awards night, Dunchurch Park Hotel, Warwickshire

Mick Ives (Team Jewson boss and ex-professional cyclist, with a multitude of National and World Masters titles to his name) is once more hosting the dinner. It is a lavish affair, with a guest speaker Geoff Cooke (ex-National track champion). The year before, it had been former Olympic Ladies Road Champion Nicole Cooke (who had won the title in Beijing in 2008; I would give her a lift back to the station in my car after the dinner–how good is that!).

Mick had raced at the top level, across a whole host of disciplines, for over fifty years and went right back to Barrie's heyday. Whilst now, he was the Director Sportiff of Team Jewson (a local concern) with a wealth of good riders. The sponsors were present at the dinner, so Mick was determined to put on a good show.

The guests hadn't arrived yet as Mick tended to all the pictures and bikes, along with the slide show that would help promote the team to the public that night. Meantime, I was busy trying to set the sound equipment up, which would help project his dulcet tones later that evening. However, as I went about my business, my mind would be in a totally different place.

Earlier that year, our Dad had died at the age of ninety. He'd had a bloody 'good inning' (as he no

112

doubt would have said) and thankfully, he'd managed to avoid going to live in a home, which he would have hated. (Okay, so he did spend an hour in one, before being taken ill and being rushed to hospital, typical Dad, stubborn till the bloody end!) So, my Dad was dead, which was bad enough in itself, and yet, it also meant that yet another link to my brother was gone.

Yet, that was then, and we were nearly ready to go. Mick had done his sound check, but as he muttered some last words towards me, I would be back in time.

"BARRIE ELSON AND MICK IVES WIN; ATKINS SECOND"

For the link, it had been restored, Mick had known my Dad for years, but more importantly, he had known Barrie at his peak. So many times, he and my brother had shared the headlines and as I looked across the table and chairs now, I could see him with Barrie once again. The Elson mythology back in the room!

With nostalgia ringing in my ears, I kept the feeling close at hand as I made small talk to people about gear ratios and bottom brackets (I didn't really). Whilst as the awards drew to a close, I (along with some of the others) would make my way to the bar for a late-night drink, ensuring that I ended up on the table that included Mick. For this was where the stories were told, where reminiscence knew no bounds, as we sat in silence, Mick's disciples, listening to him convey memories of a better day.

Although this time, however, it would be slightly different, as before he graced us with his presence I spotted an old family friend: Steve Oliver.

Steve was a fair bit older than me and had raced against Greg as a schoolboy. Why I wasn't even sure he'd ever met Barrie. But, that mattered little now, as he waxed lyrical about going around to our house in Binley Woods, all those years ago and my Mum's egg and chips. Ah yes, egg and chips, chip pan at the ready and hungry mouths to feed – job done! It was the 1960s and things were simpler. Men were men and so were the women and once more I was with Barrie again, him calling me a spoilt brat, me, probably looking towards our Mum for a suitable retort.

Although this time, Barrie didn't go out on his bike, deciding instead to stay at home, me and him bickering well into the night. While Barrie, content that he had finally put his younger brother in his place, would simply live forever.

~

I recall children playing in the wood. Barrie, Mandy and Greg, yet I see no faces. Ah Greg, he's in such boisterous mood, defiant almost, picking up a small branch and beating with it. Twack after twack, he punishes a tree with its own discarded arm. Twack after twack...until crack! An end is sent flying in the air as I go down, a head gushing with blood before...nothing.

Although, I'm awake now, thrown vigorously from side to side, and yet I feel supported, help is at hand. I look high into the vibrant sky; see bright amazing

114

sunlight cascading through a multitude of trees, blocked only by a silhouette. A silhouette of a face I cannot see. Oh, how I wish I could have seen that face, to touch it, to feel it, to greet it…for, I never got the chance to see that face again.

I was only four when Barrie died. My respect for him will last forever.

Printed in Great Britain
by Amazon